U.S. Support for UN Peacekeeping
Areas for Additional DOD Assistance

Nancy Soderberg

Center for Technology and National Security Policy

National Defense University

September 2007

Ambassador Nancy Soderberg is an author, public commentator, and Visiting Distinguished Scholar at the University of North Florida. From 2001–2005, she served as Vice President for Multilateral Affairs of the International Crisis Group in New York, a non-profit conflict prevention organization. She served in the White House as the third-ranked official on the National Security Council (1993–1996) and as Alternate Representative to the United Nations (1997–2001), with the rank of Ambassador. Prior to joining the Administration, she served as Senior Foreign Policy Advisor to Senator Edward M. Kennedy. She has been active in national politics over the last twenty years, serving in a variety of positions on the campaigns of the Democratic nominee for President.

Her first book, *The Superpower Myth: The Use and Misuse of American Might,* was published in March 2005. Her forthcoming book, *Power and Prosperity: A Better Way to Spread American Values,* is due out in 2007. She is a member of the Council on Foreign Relations, a member of the Board of Concern Worldwide, and serves on the advisory board of the National Committee on American Foreign Policy and the Tannenbaum Center. New York City Mayor Michael Bloomberg appointed her in 2002 as President of the Sister City Program of the City of New York, a position she held until January 2006. She speaks and publishes regularly in leading newspapers and journals on national security policy. She is a frequent commentator on national and international television and radio.

Defense & Technology Papers *are published by the National Defense University Center for Technology and National Security Policy, Fort Lesley J. McNair, Washington, DC. CTNSP publications are available online at* http://www.ndu.edu/ctnsp/publications.html.

Contents

Additional materials are available as appendices to the online version of this paper, which is posted on the CTNSP website at <http://www.ndu.edu/ctnsp/ Defense_Tech_Papers.htm>. Those materials include UNDKPO recommendations for additional support to the UN Police Division and prepared remarks delivered at a March 2, 2007, meeting at National Defense University and cited in this paper.

Executive Summary

Over the last decade, and particularly following the attacks of September 11, 2001, the Pentagon has increasingly viewed failed states, also referred to as "under- or ungoverned spaces," as a threat to U.S. national security and recognized the importance of peacekeeping to U.S. interests. As one senior defense official put it, "the U.S. government is committed to making peacekeeping work."[1] The 2006 Quadrennial Defense Review (QDR) states "The Department [of Defense] stands ready to increase its assistance to the United Nations Peacekeeping Operations in areas of the Department's expertise such as doctrine, training, strategic planning and management."

Yet, as the Department of Defense (DOD) recognizes the importance of under- and ungoverned spaces and the need for stability operations, it is overstretched by the war on terror and combat in Iraq and Afghanistan. Thus, any role to support peacekeeping will have to be limited and perhaps even deferred. That said, the more that can be done now, the less U.S. forces will have to do in the future. U.S. Government (USG) entities beyond DOD, particularly the Department of State (DOS) and National Security Council (NSC), must also be involved in the effort to support peacekeeping.

This report addresses primarily those areas in which limited DOD involvement will provide multiplier benefits to U.S. security. While beyond the scope of this study, a government-wide, comprehensive review of possible assistance should be conducted. It is also important to remember that DOD assistance is not a panacea for deficiencies in the United Nations Department of Peacekeeping Operations (UNDPKO) and that DOD support is "only as useful as the UN structure in which it is received."[2]

With a historical high of more than 100,000 military, police, and civilian personnel serving in the 20 current peace operations, the United Nations (UN) is second only to the United States in troops deployed.[3] In 2007, UN numbers could increase another 20–40 percent with additional troops deployed to Lebanon and East Timor, and possible new missions in Darfur, Chad/Central African Republic, and other yet unknown locations.[4] The growing number of complex missions has taxed the UN's ability to meet these challenges. The problems are particularly acute in Africa, the location of most of today's failed states and thus a growing terrorism risk.

Some major political and practical problems exist in the UN approach to peacekeeping. The mandates of peacekeeping missions are often awkward compromises, and robust enforcement mandates rare. Often the mission's host nation objects to enforcement operations or the United Nations Security Council (UNSC) mandate is ambiguous, especially regarding the protection of civilians. As a top DOD official said, "the UN needs to scale back national caveats"

---

[1] Prepared remarks of Acting Deputy Assistant Secretary of Defense for Coalition Affairs, Debra Cagan, NDU offsite, March 2, 2007 are available at <http://www.ndu.edu/ctnsp/Defense_Tech_Papers.htm>.
[2] Ibid.
[3] UNDKPO manages almost 200,000 personnel annually given rotations, new hires, and turnover. Of the 20 missions, several are managed by the Department of Political Affairs, including the missions in Afghanistan and Iraq. There were 10 UN missions in 2001.
[4] Email exchange with UNDPKO official, April 20, 2007.

and include "all necessary means" as vital language to the mission. Otherwise, factions take advantage of a weak mandate.[5]

The UN tradition of seeking to be impartial in its mandate, driven largely out of a desire not to become involved in the conflict or because of pressure from states involved, has often led to weak responses when challenged by militias. The robust mandate of the strengthened peacekeeping operation in Lebanon can serve as a new standard for mandates. UN officials stress that the UN cannot rectify a fundamental breakdown in a peace process and that it is important to be clear about what a peacekeeping operation can and cannot achieve.[6]

Member states need to recognize that peacekeeping is a permanent need for the foreseeable future and must change their approach and begin to invest in a sustainable system that will support current and future peacekeeping needs. Just as the United States is seeking to strengthen its own capabilities in peacekeeping and peacebuilding, so, too, is the UN. The United States can play an important role in building international support to help the UN build up such permanent capacities.

UNDPKO certainly welcomes additional U.S. support, especially as it expands and reorganizes its military staff. One key requirement for DOD is that any DOD personnel assigned to the UN be placed in positions of real authority in headquarters and in the field, a point UNDPKO readily accepts. However, certain sensitivities must be recognized. As one UNDPKO official cautioned, DOD support is welcome but it "needs to be carefully managed and balanced with our need to reflect the balance of the UN membership and in particular the perspectives of the Troop Contributing Countries (TCC). . . . This is particularly so in light of the sensitivities with regard to what might be perceived as an effort to link U.S. counter-terrorism strategies and UN peacekeeping."[7] That said, the UN cannot have U.S. support both ways, wanting more support but only if it is not visible.[8]

There are also significant political obstacles to DOD's providing more assistance to the UN from four key areas: the Administration, Congress, the DOD bureaucracies, and UN member states. Overcoming these obstacles will take strong, visionary DOD leadership and advocacy. However, it is important to recognize that any contributions to the UN are only as effective as the UN itself is effective. The UN can greatly benefit from direct support from DOD in the key areas outlined in this study, and the United States can benefit as well.

Of particular importance is the need for an initiative to work with international partners to respond to peacekeeping requests in a systematic way and strengthen an international peacekeeping coordination and support mechanism that would better match needs with resources. U.S. forces must also participate more directly in UN headquarters and UN peacekeeping operations in the field. Such key staff support would provide much needed expertise and key links back to the Pentagon, and might also encourage other TCCs to participate. For DOD to provide such assistance, it must see the UN as key to the Global War on Terror (GWOT) and support it accordingly. While the United States tends to be the first port of call for many requests (not least because of its expertise in maintaining forces overseas), other

---

[5] Prepared remarks of LTG Walter "Skip" Sharp, Director of the Joint Staff, NDU offsite, March 2, 2007 available at <http://www.ndu.edu/ctnsp/Defense_Tech_Papers.htm>.

[6] Prepared remarks of UN Under-Secretary-General for Peacekeeping Operations, Jean-Marie Guéhenno, NDU offsite, March 2, 2007 available at <http://www.ndu.edu/ctnsp/Defense_Tech_Papers.htm>.

[7] Email exchange, UNDPKO official, February 27, 2007.

[8] Sharp remarks.

nations can provide much of the necessary assistance. A strong leadership role can help galvanize others to participate, relieving some pressure for U.S. assistance.

Given the recent USG decision to establish a new combatant command, U.S. Africa Command (AFRICOM), UN officials are especially interested in future U.S. support to African peacekeeping forces and regional structures.[9] The establishment of AFRICOM offers a unique opportunity for the United States to help galvanize international support for peacekeeping, and a new opportunity for close U.S. partnership with the United Nations.

While outside the scope of this study, the way the interagency process handles peacekeeping affects overall U.S. support to the UN and deserves attention. Something as simple as educating elements of the USG on what the UN is doing would help.[10] Peacekeeping support is hampered by the lack of full implementation of the December 7, 2005 National Security Presidential Directive (NSPD) 44. NSPD 44 recognizes the need to coordinate, strengthen, and harmonize reconstruction and stabilization efforts with U.S. military plans and operations. Most of the coordination is carried out in the field between the Ambassador and combatant commander, which generally works well, but little interagency coordination occurs back in Washington.[11] For instance, the Policy Coordination Committee (PCC) for Reconstruction and Stabilization Operations set up to coordinate stabilization efforts has not fully done so. The Office of the Coordinator for Reconstruction and Stabilization at the Department of State (DOS), created in August 2004 to assist states in transition, has yet to fulfill that purpose. Senior-level attention to ensure full implementation of NSPD 44 would assist in overall USG efforts to support peacekeeping.

Coordination is also a problem. There is, for instance, no central database or tracking system to handle incoming offers of financial, material, and personnel support. The U.S. government is uniquely qualified to assist in a coordination role, perhaps working with outside contractors.

In addition, the plethora of U.S. peacekeeping and counterterrorism efforts that have developed over the years has never been rationalized, coordinated, or reviewed comprehensively. DOS and DOD both train and equip troops abroad. While the purposes often differ, their goals are often the same—to leave behind forces capable of protecting borders and maintaining stability. Both departments have a variety of antiterrorism programs that overlap among themselves and also with efforts to train peacekeepers. In addition, U.S. anti-terror and peacekeeping programs also overlap with many international efforts. A strategic review and rationalization of these efforts would be beneficial.

Much has already been done to implement the May 2006 Building Partnership Capacity QDR Execution Roadmap. One of the key goals is to build partner capabilities and develop collaborative mechanisms to reduce the drivers of instability. DOD is already considering ways it can assist UNDPKO in such areas as strategic planning, doctrine development, education and training, and executive management. It is also considering ways for advising, training, and providing personnel support to the UNDPKO military planning office. The report offers broad

---

[9] The new African combatant command, AFRICOM, should be fully operational by October 2008, with the headquarters stood up by October 2007, initially in Stuttgart, Germany. Comment made by DOD official at NDU offsite, March 2, 2007.

[10] Suggestion of Acting DASD Cagan, March 2, 2007.

[11] Some believe that DOD and DOS do not have good interagency coordination on who needs training and equipping and that COCOMs and DOS have different priorities. Comments of DOD and PKSOI staff, NDU offsite, March 2, 2007.

recommendations to assist UN peacekeeping efforts, as well as specific short- and long-term steps to be considered.

Five Broad Steps DOD Should Take to Further Assist the UN

First, the USG should develop and support a new coordination mechanism: a coalition of states constituting a "Core Group of Support to Peace Operations" (a "Core Group") to press for UNDPKO reform and coordinated assistance. Included should be some combination of: the five permanent members of the UN Security Council (P-5); TCC (and potential future ones); key regional organizations such as the African Union (AU), North Atlantic Treaty Organization (NATO), European Union (EU), and Standby High Readiness Brigade (SHIRBRIG); along with the involvement of the International Association of Peace Training Centers. With strong U.S. leadership, the group should help create a central database and tracking system to manage incoming offers of financial, material, and personnel support as well as training of troops. As part of this effort, the Core Group would respond to UNDPKO requests in a systematic way, with the United States taking on some tasks, while pressing other nations to take on some as well. How the UN might best assist Africa, utilizing the new African combatant command (AFRICOM) could perhaps serve as an initial focus of the Core Group.

Second, DOD should selectively increase U.S. participation in the UN command structure. Recognizing the military needs of the UN are expanding, UNDPKO intends to increase its military positions, thereby facilitating the placement of more U.S. personnel in the department. Also, the more resources the United States provides the UN, the easier it is to second more officers. At UNDPKO Headquarters (HQ) in New York, DOD should press for an increase in the number of seconded billets, mainly as military planners but also more broadly to assist the UN (and DOD) develop expertise. In the field, DOD should provide more personnel to strategic headquarter positions, administrative positions, specialized enabling skills, police missions, and observation roles. While DOD believes it can succeed in securing at most two military staff positions at UN HQ, UN officials indicate more might be possible. UNDPKO must ensure any such staff is placed in real value-added positions.

Third, the United States and UN should explore additional ways to include UN officials and peacekeeping troops in ongoing activities, especially U.S. training exercises and lessons learned efforts. While DOD is already active in many regional organizations, it should consider more active engagement in African, Latin American, and Asian organizations to help achieve and coordinate an international architecture to support peacekeeping. Deployment of DOD military officers and civilian personnel to UN and regional training centers should also be considered, as they would serve as important multipliers. New opportunities for partnerships, such as one between AFRICOM and the new National Security University, should be fully explored. Trilateral dialogues with the United States, UN, and key potential African partners should be considered. A UN liaison to AFRICOM should be considered.

Fourth, the United States and UN should press for formal inclusion of UN peacekeeping missions in the agendas of the G-8 summit meetings. Given the importance of peacekeeping in meeting today's threats, as well as the wide variety of needs, the issue must be addressed at the highest levels of those with the most to offer.

Fifth, there needs to be more consistent, high-level dialogue on UN needs and how to meet them. One option to achieve that goal would be annual or semi-annual offsite senior-level strategic dialogues such as the one hosted by the National Defense University (NDU) March 2,

2007. NDU stands ready to host more such events. A regular UN "wish-list" for USG consideration might also be helpful.

The report also offers specific recommendations for the short and longer term, primarily for DOD but also for overall USG policy toward UNDPKO.

Five Short-Term Steps

Strategic planning. Provide UNDPKO assistance to develop further planning doctrine on strategic issues versus field/theatre level activities. DOD military planners should be made available on an ad hoc and temporary basis to address the surge capacity need, mostly through the U.S. Mission to the United Nations (USUN). Developing ways to make lessons learned more actionable and more quickly implemented, as well as developing a U.S.–UN sharing mechanism, would be useful. Long-term contingency planning and better sharing of intelligence also should be considered, including a resumption of the briefings of officials from key missions and the UN by the National Intelligence Council (NIC). Such assistance could be done by DOD, through the peacekeeping institutes, or in concert with NATO or the EU, and other regional organizations. Intelligence done at the operational level as part of force protection might ease some of the political difficulties involved. As AFRICOM is established, the United States and the UN should establish ways to assist the AU develop its peacekeeping capabilities, perhaps using the Core Group.

Doctrine. DOD should continue to develop and share with UNDPKO peacekeeping guidance framework in the areas identified by UNDPKO: policy directives, standard operating procedures, manuals, and guidelines. The United States and UN should find a mechanism to share the lessons learned in real time and also share exercises to build doctrine at the operational and strategic levels to build horizontal links at the tactical level, such as between the police and military. DOD also could help promote standardized international peacekeeping doctrine through the various regional peacekeeping centers. Should the new National Security University become a reality, it would provide a good opportunity for the United States to work with the UN and other partners in the future. Annual meetings among key players in UNDPKO, DOS, DOD, and regional organizations should be initiated to assist in developing and implementing doctrine.

Management. An interagency working group should be established to assist the UN in each of its five tasks and to work closely with UNDPKO's cross-disciplinary Task Force and working groups in each of the five areas identified as priorities by the UN. The USG also should continue to press for an internal DKPO auditor (separate from the Office of Internal Oversight Services (OIOS)) to enhance compliance of UN Missions with UN standards, once they are articulated in doctrinal materials. UNDKPO officials indicate openness to this step. Such a step would be useful in addition to the establishment of the Evaluations Section currently pending with the General Assembly.

Training. DOD should provide a variety of training and encourage others, especially the Europeans, to take responsibility for certain areas either through the EU or NATO. Areas to be considered include: integrated training services, up-to-date training curricula for priority operational and specialist areas, and ongoing support and training of such personnel in between deployments to assist in the retention of personnel. Force protection is increasingly important. Bilateral relationships are the most effective way to train and equip. An African training hub also would be useful. Achieving sustainability, especially through annual training exercises and senior leadership instruction, will be key. DOD should direct that the U.S. Army Peacekeeping and Stability Operations Institute (PKSOI), in conjunction with other regional training centers, participate in the development of annual exercises for UNDKPO personnel and TCC troops.

Police. While not part of the four areas identified by the QDR, police assistance should also be considered. As demands expand, UNDPKO will require additional assistance in the Police Division and in expanding the Standing Police Capacity. For Formed Police Units (FPUs) to be fully operational, such units must have adequate and appropriate personal and collective police equipment and self-sustaining capabilities. While assisting police is primarily a DOS function, DOD also has capabilities of potential use to the UN, such as crowd control, basic training, infrastructure building, contingency planning, maintaining a roster (DOS) of assistance in overall police training, coordination, and doctrine development. UN participation in U.S. training sessions on law and order techniques, including on-line courses, should be considered.

Five Longer-Term Issues

Equipment. DOD should evaluate whether to seek a change in authorities to enable it to leave key equipment behind to the recipients of peacekeeping exercises. Ways to address DOS foreign policy issues also must be found. The United States and UN should press the Europeans to do more, including tapping into Cold War stocks, either through the EU or NATO. A more significant Brindisi-type stockpile facility in West Africa also should be established.

Funding problems. The USG must make funding a priority, stressing its role in the war on terrorism, making it clear it is a central part of the post 9/11 war on terrorism. All United Nations Security Council (UNSC)-blessed peacekeeping missions, including regional ones, should be funded by assessed contributions.

Rapid deployment reserve. The UN continues to seek to build up a reserve capacity to deploy military capabilities rapidly. The idea remains very controversial in the USG, in Congress, and with other potential contributors, but it deserves further discussion and study, perhaps including support for the concept, with others providing the capacity. UNDKPO has suggested that DOD support efforts to revise its UN Standby Arrangement Systems and use the Core Group to promote sign up by countries concerned.

Enabling capacities. DOD could provide some enabling capacities and seek lead nations to provide assistance in remaining areas. It should seek key hubs for support to UN missions and regional forces, especially in Africa.

Expanding and strengthening UN certified programs. Continuing to work with partner organizations (Challenges, Conference of American Armies, International Association of Peace Training Centers, G-8 Global Peacekeeping Operations Initiative) and allies to encourage the expanded use of such standard training should be considered. Promoting these standards through regional peacekeeping missions also should be considered as well as inviting key peacekeeping officials at the UN and regional organizations to participate in U.S. War Colleges and other educational opportunities.

Four Areas for Further Study

Conduct a comprehensive Review. A comprehensive interagency review of current U.S. support to international peacekeeping would help the USG determine what works, what does not work, and what is missing.

Rationalize and coordinate peacekeeping and terrorism functions, including training and equipping efforts. To implement fully NSPD 44, the interagency process must decide if the authorities under Sections 1206 and 1207 of the National Defense Authorization Act will be permanent. Ultimately, an interagency decision on a division of roles between DOS and DOD is needed.

Help support coordinated worldwide peacekeeping improvements, especially in Africa. Take the lead in pressing for partnerships to support the Africa Action Plan and the African Standby Force. The new AFRICOM provides an excellent opportunity to integrate U.S. and UN efforts in Africa, as well as to press for Europeans to do more to help African peacekeepers. One key goal would be to build a permanent strategic headquarters or secretariat within the regional and/or sub-regional organizations that could support peacekeeping operations, particularly in doctrines and procedures.

Review the role of private contractors. A USG-wide review of contractor performance and the development of standards, rules, and codes of conduct would be worthwhile.

Introduction

The 2006 Quadrennial Defense Review (QDR) states that "The [Defense] Department stands ready to increase its assistance to the United Nations Peacekeeping Operations in areas of the Department's expertise such as doctrine, training, strategic planning and management." This study evaluates first the needs of the United Nations Department of Peacekeeping Operations (UNDPKO) and next suggest ways the Department of Defense (DOD) can assist the United Nations (UN) in meeting them. An analysis of key political challenges in Washington and the UN is also included.

The specific tasks of the study are:

- Review and assess DOD capabilities to provide assistance in areas of deficiencies identified in the QDR. The study identifies additional areas for consideration, particularly those within the five goals identified by the UN. Civilian and military roles are included in the review and assessment.
- Review and assess the political obstacles in the UN and in Washington that must be overcome for DOD to provide such enabling capabilities and assess whether the U.S.-UN relationship needs adjusting.
- Develop recommendations for provision of DOD assistance to the UN in areas of its expertise, including perhaps through regional organizations such as the African Union (AU), European Union (EU), or North Atlantic Treaty Organization (NATO). Ways the United States might attract participation of untapped resources for UN operations also is included.
- Develop areas for further study.

As part of this study, NDU convened an offsite with key UN and USG officials involved in peacekeeping March 2, 2007. The meeting contributed substantially to this report and reaffirmed the commitment of both to work together to improve UN peacekeeping. The UN is looking for partnerships and believes one with the United States would be of "fundamental importance."[12] DOD is committed to assisting UN peacekeeping and is open to new proposals and ideas. This study seeks to offer ideas to both the UN and DOD on how they can best build such a partnership.

Over the last decade, and particularly following the 9/11 attacks, DOD has increasingly viewed failed states, also called "under- or ungoverned spaces," as a threat to U.S. national security and accepted the importance of peacekeeping for U.S. interests. As former Secretary of Defense Donald Rumsfeld stated in fall 2005, "If there's anything that's clear in the 21st century it's that the world needs peacekeepers."[13] A variety of programs have emerged to address states' abilities to assist foreign troops in conducting peacekeeping missions. There is a growing understanding that the more others can take on this task, the less will be the burden on U.S. troops. Yet as DOD recognizes the importance of under- and ungoverned spaces and the need for stability operations, its ability to participate generously in UN peacekeeping is restricted by its obligations in the war on terror, Iraq, and Afghanistan. Thus any role in supporting peacekeeping will have to be limited and perhaps not even undertaken in the near term. That said, the more that can be done now, the less U.S. forces will have to do in the future. This report seeks to

---

[12] Guéhenno remarks.

[13] Statement delivered at a news conference in Ulan Bator, Mongolia, October 22, 2005. Cited at <http://www.msnbc.msn.com/id/9735858/>.

recommend those areas in which limited DOD involvement will provide multiplier benefits to U.S. security.

The QDR recognizes that DOD cannot meet many of today's challenges alone and that success requires working in close cooperation with allies and partners abroad, including the UN. UN operations also are more economical. UN operations cost only half what U.S. operations do – and the United States pays only 25 percent of that lower cost.[14] However, UN missions are less effective in certain areas, especially enforcement. Still, UN peacekeeping efforts are central to and should be considered an important part of the Global War on Terrorism (GWOT).

With nearly 100,000 military, police, and civilian personnel serving in the 20 current peace operations, the UN is second only to the U.S. in troops deployed.[15] Yet the vast number of complex missions and their rapid increase (from 10 in 2001 to in 2006) has taxed the UN's ability to meet these challenges. The problems are particularly acute in Africa, the location of most of today's failed states and thus a growing terrorism risk. Unlike most other regions, Africa lacks capable troops to address its many crises. The failures of the AU force in Darfur underscore the deficiencies in that body's ability to deploy and sustain forces, while the refusal of the government of Sudan to permit a more capable UN force is a stark reminder of the limits on UN political power.

Today, more than 75 percent of UN peacekeepers are in Africa, with recent difficult missions in Burundi, Liberia, Cote d'Ivoire, and Sudan, as well as a tripling of the forces in the Democratic Republic of Congo (DRC).[16] Such crises have placed increasing demands on DOD. DOD's decision to establish a new Africa command based on the continent will, among other things, go far to better assist the various peacekeeping and anti-terrorism efforts resulting from the increased demands placed on DOD by such crises.[17]

UNDPKO manages 20 operations and is planning potential expansions and additional missions. Yet, it faces a variety of problems, including: lack of global coordinating mechanisms; a lack of well-trained, well-equipped troops; poor intelligence on events on the ground and over the horizon; increasing threats to its personnel on the ground; and repeated shortages in the $5 billion peacekeeping budget (which represents roughly 0.5 percent of global military spending).[18] UN budget problem are caused by political problems with member states, primarily the United States, which uses its funding as leverage to press for important and much needed reforms.[19] High turnover rates in peacekeeping missions hamper effectiveness, creating a 30–40 percent vacancy rate.[20]

---

[14] Dobbins, James, et al., *The UN's Role in Nation-Building from the Congo to Iraq*, RAND Corporation, 2005, Santa Monica, CA. It is important to keep in mind, however, that some support costs are not factored in.

[15] <http://www.un.org/Depts/dpko/dpko/bnote.htm>. These figures include the total number of personnel serving in 15 peacekeeping operations and three UNDPKO-led special political and/or peace building missions—UNAMA (Afghanistan), UNIOSIL (Sierra Leone), and BINUM (Burundi). Two other political missions (brining total missions to 20) are UNAMI in Iraq (with 223 troops and 7 military observers) and UNMIN in Nepal (with 86 military observers) as of March 2007. The mission in East Timor is transitioning to a full peacekeeping mission once again. Total authorized is about 100,000 personnel. In addition to the 90,263 personnel in UNDPKO missions, another 2556 are in the Department of Political Affairs missions managed by UNDPKO.

[16] For an excellent review of African peacekeeping efforts, see Testimony by Victoria K. Holt, The Henry L. Stimson Center, Hearing on "African Organizations and Institutions: Positive Cross-Continental Progress," Subcommittee on African Affairs, Senate Foreign Relations Committee, November 17, 2005.

[17] Email exchange with DOD official, May 9, 2007.

[18] <http://www.un.org/Depts/dpko/factsheet.pdf>.

[19] According to a former senior UNDPKO military planner, "the shortages are mainly in the assessed budget—PKO and the immediate effect is delays in reimbursements to the TCCs, which has an impact on their willingness to

The UN could greatly benefit from direct support from the Pentagon in the key areas outlined in this study. Most important is the need for an initiative to work with international partners to respond to peacekeeping requests in a systematic way and strengthen an international peacekeeping coordination Core Group that helps match needs with the world's resources. Second is the need for U.S. forces to participate more directly in UN HQ and UN peacekeeping operations in the field. Such key staff support would provide much needed expertise and key links back to the Pentagon, and perhaps encourage other Troop Contributing Countries (TCCs) to participate as well. As one UN official put it, we need "people and systems."[21] For DOD to provide such assistance, it must see the UN as key to GWOT and support it accordingly.

Some Pentagon officials argue that the UN should close some of its peacekeeping missions, especially some that are nearly half a century old. Yet such decisions are beyond the remit of the UN staff. Support for continuing such missions is driven by the parties involved, with the support of the UNSC. Any mission closures would have to involve a strong U.S.-led diplomatic effort within the specific regions. A second voiced concern is over the failure of the UN to quickly reimburse member states that contribute troops. Previously, states complained of the problem to Secretary of Defense Rumsfeld.[22] It must be recognized that the arcane nature of the UN budget process must be reformed; however, it also must be recognized that the United States itself causes many of the UN's budget problems by placing caps on funding and failing to pay assessed dues on time and in full. The current U.S. arrears of about $400 million are likely to increase this year, given the increased missions in Lebanon, Sudan, East Timor, and the DRC.[23]

Some in Washington complain that the UN consistently plans for worst-case scenarios, driving requested troop numbers higher than necessary. UN officials counter that the UNSC, particularly the United States, often pushes for a reduction in numbers without any reduction in tasks. "We are pushed to do things on the cheap," said one senior UNDPKO official.[24] In addition, political pressures to keep the number of troops down for budgetary reasons inhibit the UN from acting on a worst-case scenario.[25] Some Pentagon officials urge the UN to offer options for peacekeeping tasks. UN officials have agreed they could offer a range of tasks with corresponding troop requirements from which the UNSC could choose, making decisions on a task-to-troop basis. But they were also adamant about the need to plan for the worst-case scenario, claiming that failure to do so was one of the most costly mistakes of the 1990s.

One problem mentioned by UN officials is that member states still see peacekeeping as temporary, which is "wrong for an investment strategy."[26] Member states need to recognize that

---

continue or increase the levels of staff officers and troops provided. TCCs blame the United States for their late payments, but the UN system is partly responsible too." Email exchange September 29, 2006.

[20] Email exchange with senior UN military planner, August 11, 2006. A former senior UNDPKO military planner also suggested vacancy rates are particularly problematic regarding the civilian components of UN missions, mainly due to a slow and tedious hiring process. "The turnover rates among key staff officers is high—six months is the typical tour demanded by France, Canada, UK, United States, and others. Among the TCCs, most are on annual rotations." Email exchange September 29, 2006.

[21] Interview with senior UN official, June 28, 2006.

[22] Both concerns were raised by a senior DOD official in an interview June 14, 2006.

[23] Costs of the UN missions for the 2006-07 period could go as high as $6.1 billion, of which the United States would be assessed $1.6 billion. See The Partnership for Effective Peacekeeping, <http://www.effectivepeacekeeping.org>.

[24] Interview with senior UN official June 6, 2006.

[25] One UN official cited the small number of troops in the DRC and Sudan as examples. Email exchange August 25, 2006.

[26] Interview with senior UN official, June 28, 2006.

peacekeeping is a permanent need for the foreseeable future and that states must change their approach and begin to invest in a sustainable system that will support current and future peacekeeping needs. Just as the United States is seeking to strengthen its own capabilities in peacekeeping and peacebuilding, so, too, is the UN. The United States can play an important role in building international support to help the UN build up such permanent capacities.

One area that needs further recognition is the vast number of civil political activities of the UN and how they fit into peacekeeping activities. Peacekeeping is often seen only through the lens of the UNDPKO and not, as one UN official puts it, "in terms of the integrated UN approach that is increasingly influencing our approach to postconflict peace operations."[27] Recently Undersecretary General Ibrahim Gambari of the Department of Political Affairs stated, "Stemming armed conflicts before they erupt requires a bigger investment in preventive action—not just lofty rhetoric to that effect."[28]

As the recent establishment of the UN's Peace Building Commission recognizes, conflict prevention and containment involve a broad range of assistance to civil society institutions, as well as sustained international development assistance. For instance, UN efforts to assist in elections, draft constitutions, assist in the rule of law, and address the needs of women all impact societies in transition. Any comprehensive approach to peacekeeping support must address how these programs can best be integrated with those efforts.

While any detailed analysis of the issue is beyond the scope of this study, it is important to recognize that the USG interagency process needs improvement and other departments beyond DOD can do more to assist UN peacekeeping. Within the U.S. government, peacekeeping support is hampered by a failure to fully implement the December 7, 2005 National Security Presidential Directive (NSPD) 44. The directive recognizes the need to coordinate, strengthen, and harmonize reconstruction and stabilization efforts with U.S. military plans and operations. Yet the Policy Coordination Committee (PCC) for Reconstruction and Stabilization Operations set up to implement NSPD 44 has failed to do so. In addition, the lack of support to the Office of the Coordinator for Reconstruction and Stabilization at DOS (S/CRS), created in August 2004 to assist states in transition, must be addressed. The purpose of the office, yet unfulfilled, is to institutionalize the capacity in the U.S. government to draw on capabilities across the civilian world and provide liaison, coordination, and oversight to civilian and military operations.[29] S/CRS now has a set of triggers and operational models, including a command and control apparatus, representatives at COCOMs, and specialists in the field who integrate policy with the military. S/CRS is already doing planning for Kosovo.[30] AFRICOM may offer new opportunities for S/CRS. Senior-level attention is urgently needed to ensure full implementation of NSPD 44.

The U.S. Agency for International Development (USAID) has developed a "fragile state" strategy and now has an office of military operations that will coordinate with DOD. The office has developed a framework that looks at both stabilization and reconstruction and is now testing it across the combatant commands (COCOMs) and on the civilian world in Sudan and Haiti.[31] DOD Directive 3000.05 of November 2005 provides guidance on DOD stability operations. It recognizes that "stability operations are a core U.S. military mission that the Department of

---

[27] Email exchange with UN official, August 25, 2006.

[28] Taken from the press conference by Department of Political Affairs concerning Secretary-General's Report on Conflict Prevention, September 6, 2006.

[29] Interestingly, this is exactly what UNDPKO is seeking to do.

[30] Comments by John Herbst, S/SCR Coordinator, during NDU offsite.

[31] Carlos Pascual, former Director of S/CRS, now at the Brookings Institution, *Joint Force Quarterly,* Summer, 2006.

Defense shall be prepared to conduct and support. They shall be given priority comparable to combat operations."[32] COCOMs remain the focal point for DOD execution of the Directive and are in charge of conducting exercises and bilateral training.

On paper, there is a system to address the new challenges of peacekeeping, peacebuilding, and stabilization offices. On paper, there is also a clear division of labor between DOS, USAID, and DOD. But in practice, the system is not working. Rivalries between DOD and DOS and continued tension over the appropriate division of responsibility between the role of S/CRS and USAID undermine the U.S. government's ability to support peacekeeping activities. The administration has failed to provide senior-level attention to the office or the resources to make it effective. Congressional support for the office does not exist either. The administration must decide to support S/CRS. Otherwise, it is likely to disappear or become simply a clearinghouse for conflict and emergency personnel.

The new arrangements in Sections 1206 and 1207 of the 2006 National Defense Authorization Act that provide for DOD funding of peacekeeping and anti-terror programs must also be addressed. These authorities address the need to provide urgent funding but fail to address the underlying issue of which authorities best lie in DOS or DOD. Some in DOS and Congress have expressed concern about what they perceive as DOD encroachment into foreign policy. They argue that decisions on training and equipping, whether in a peacekeeping or counter-terrorism context, should be made in the context of international foreign policy and bilateral relationships. They are concerned about power over foreign policy decisions shifting to the Pentagon. In its defense, DOD seeks to coordinate closely all such decisions and maintains its role is appropriate, given the lack of DOS funds to carry out such activities. An interagency review of the current roles and a clearer division of authorities and budgets could ease some of the current tension.

In addition, an interagency review of the peacekeeping and counterterrorism efforts that have developed over the years would help ensure a rational division of labor among the departments, minimizing duplication and ensuring that needs are met. U.S. anti-terror and peacekeeping programs also overlap with a plethora of international efforts that need similar coordination and rationalization. A strategic review and rationalization of these efforts is needed. A "Core Group of Support to Peace Operations" (the "Core Group") could help press for UNDPKO reform and support and coordinate international peacekeeping assistance.

Such a group has been useful in other circumstances in building political support (for instance, in Afghanistan before 9/11 and the Balkans in the 1990s), coordinating requests for assistance, and building support for states to meet such needs. In this case, some combination of the P-5, TCCs (and potential future ones), key regional organizations (AU, NATO, EU, and Standby High Readiness Brigade (SHIRBRIG), along with the involvement of the International Association of Peace Training Centers should be considered. With strong U.S. leadership, the Core Group should help create a central database and tracking system to manage incoming offers of financial, material, and personnel support as well as training of troops. As part of this effort, the Core Group would respond to UNDPKO requests in a systematic way, with the United States taking on some tasks, while pressing other nations to take on other key tasks. Building support for the African Union, working with the new AFRICOM, could be a useful first focus of the Core Group.

---

[32] See section 4.1 of DOD Directive 3000.5.

Building Partnership Capacity

The May 2006 Building Partnership Capacity QDR Execution Roadmap (the Roadmap) states as a key goal building partner capabilities and developing collaborative mechanisms to reduce the drivers of instability.[33] "This means that the Department must be prepared to grow a new team of leaders and operators . . . operating alongside or within UN organizations . . . to further U.S. and partner interests."[34] The roadmap tasks DOD with developing and experimenting with a joint concept for strategic partnerships to extend governance to under- or ungoverned areas. The Roadmap also asks for a plan of action for generating a DOD capability to enable strategic partnerships to extend governance to under- and ungoverned areas, including security, economy and infrastructure, political institutions, and rule of law.[35] As the UN assists countries make the transition from conflict to sustainable peacebuilding and development, it should be considered a partner to DOD in these tasks. Thus, once these action plans are developed, they may be shared with the UN and other partners.

The QDR recognizes that under- and ungoverned spaces represent a potential security threat to the United States, and UN peacekeeping missions are designed to assist such spaces. Current U.S. policy is to protect U.S. interests while "developing the capacities of nations to more effectively address security and stability challenges."[36] The Roadmap recognizes that international organizations can operate in conjunction with, or instead of, U.S. forces and pledges to work to improve the capabilities and capacities of international organizations to conduct stabilization, security, transition and reconstruction (SSTR) operations "in order to enhance their prospects for mission success and reduce the burden on U.S. forces."[37] Several specific capabilities outlined in the Roadmap involve current UN-related roles, such as the capability to defeat terrorist networks, shape the choices of countries at strategic crossroads, prevent hostile states and non-state actors from acquiring or using weapons of mass destruction (WMD), conduct SSTR operations, and enable host countries to provide good governance.[38]

The Roadmap asks for a plan of action for DOD assistance to the UNDPKO in areas such as strategic planning, doctrine development, education and training, and executive management. It asks that the plan consider ways for advising, training, and providing personnel support to the UNDPKO military planning office.[39] It is hoped that this study will provide DOD with assistance and fresh thinking in that task.

A wide variety of excellent studies already exist on what type of assistance the UN needs to better perform in its peacekeeping role.[40] As one UN official put it, "we are overwhelmed with

---

[33] The Irregular Warfare Roadmap also addresses counterterrorism efforts that could be used to support peacekeeping efforts. This report, however, focuses on the Building Partnership Capability (BPC) roadmap as more directly relating to UN peacekeeping.

[34] BPC, QDR Execution Roadmap, May 2006, section 2.3.2.

[35] Ibid., section 3.3.4-5.

[36] From the written statement of General James L. Jones, USMC, Commander United States European Command, before the Senate Foreign Relations Committee September 28, 2005. His statements are referring to Africa.

[37] QDR Execution Roadmap, May 2006, section 4.4.1.

[38] Ibid., section 1.3.3.

[39] Op cit., QDR Executive Roadmap, section 4.4.4.

[40] For example see the Report of the Special Committee on Peacekeeping operations and its Working Group at the 2006 substantive session, the *Annual Review of Global Peace Operations 2006* produced by the New York University Center on International Cooperation, the Report of the Panel on United Nations Peace Operations by Lakhdar Brahimi from 2000, the *Future of Peace Operations* Project at the Henry L. Stimson Center, and The Challenges Project, *Meeting the Challenges of Peace Operations: Cooperation and Coordination*, Phase II Concluding Report 2003-2006, Elanders Gotab, 2005. Available at <www.challengesproject.net>.

good ideas. What we need is coordination and partners."[41] This study seeks to avoid rehashing well-covered ground. Rather it seeks to offer USG leadership concrete recommendations of ways and areas in which the Pentagon can assist UN peacekeeping operations. The study is divided into four sections that address UNDPKO needs, political obstacles to DOD Assistance to UNDPKO, recommendations, and areas for further study.

---

[41] Interview with senior UN official, June 6, 2006.

Current Needs of the UN Department of Peacekeeping Operations

In his March 2005 report, *In Larger Freedom,* UN Secretary General Kofi Annan said the "time is now ripe for a decisive move forward: the establishment of an interlocking system of peacekeeping capacities that will enable the United Nations to work with relevant regional organizations in predictable and reliable partnership."[42] Progress has been made, but only with greatly enhanced assistance from capable nations will the UN achieve that goal.

Six years after the Brahimi Report on reform of peacekeeping operations, UNDPKO continues to recognize the need for further reform and adaptation to evolving challenges. Improvements in the performance of peacekeeping have been stronger than those in peacebuilding efforts. Progress to date, including a doubling of the UN HQ staff, are enabling the UN to better plan and implement large, complex missions. The structure and organization of logistic and field support has improved. The creation of a Peacebuilding Commission and a Peace Support Office will further help UNDPKO manage and coordinate missions. The Best Practices Unit has improved and is providing important analyses. Not yet implemented are the recommendations for a central strategic planning and analysis staff and a more systematic inter-department approach to mission planning.[43]

However, based on the global situation of 2007 and the ongoing requests for UNDPKO services, the recommendations in the Brahimi Report are not ambitious enough to tackle current demands on UNDPKO. UNDPKO describes itself as "overstretched," noting that the reforms of the Brahimi Report were intended to give the UN the capacity to launch one large peace operation a year. In 2004 alone, the UN launched four large operations and is now managing complex missions in the DRC, Liberia, Cote d'Ivoire, and Sudan, and potentially another one in Darfur. The field personnel have increased more than five-fold since 2000, with a current headquarters staff-to-field personnel ratio of 1 to 137. That ratio is likely to increase as new and expanded missions develop.

To further the Brahimi reforms, the UN has placed more emphasis on improving performance in peacekeeping, including improvements in doctrine, guidance on behavior of personnel in the field, and enhanced personnel briefs prior to deployment. More progress is needed in the full range of peacebuilding activities. In 2005, the UN put forward its Peace Operations 2010 plan. It proposed a broad series of reforms to peacekeeping operations, including five goals to be achieved by 2010 in the areas of people, doctrine, partnerships, resources, and management. To implement this plan, the UNDPKO has established a cross-disciplinary Task Force and working groups in each of the five areas.

UNDPKO has continued to evolve and change to meet the challenges it has faced and continues to face in the years since the Brahimi Report was issued. The new Secretary General, Ban Ki-moon, has proposed a consolidation of responsibility, authority, and resources for all aspects of the planning and conduct of UN peacekeeping operations and related field operations. He has proposed the establishment of two specialized but tightly integrated departments to

---

[42] Report of the Secretary-General, *In Larger Freedom: Towards Security, Development and Human Rights for All,* para. 112, March 21, 2005, A/59, 2005.
[43] A/55/305-S/2000/809. See also The Challenges Project, 37, and Durch, W. J. and V.K. Holt, et al., *The Brahimi Report and the Future of UN Peace Operations* (Washington, DC.: The Henry L. Stimson Center, 2003)

manage this task: the Department of Peace Operations and the Department of Field Support. The plan will reinforce efforts to put in place integrated mission-planning processes to guide integrated teams.

The UN faces major challenges as its peacekeeping operations continue to grow, with the threats to its forces getting more diverse and dangerous. The UN is looking for assistance, particularly through partnerships. UNDPKO recognizes there "is a strategic dimension to this . . . [because] ungoverned spaces are important. Africa, in particular, is moving from warlords out to enrich themselves to the kind of ideological violence that plagues the Middle East." In this new environment, the UN is trying to be adaptable and open to different kinds of models. The UN recognizes there are three levels of forces in the world, the United States, NATO and other equivalent levels of forces, and the developing world. "There is a lot to be gained by a dialogue between all three."[44] Thus, the UN is constantly updating its doctrine, standards, and UNDKPO structure.

As UN Under-Secretary-General for Peacekeeping Operations Jean-Marie Guéhenno said, "If we are to manage our current tasks, and potentially take on new ones in 2007, we urgently require the reinforcement of planning, management and, operational capacities across the span of UN peacekeeping."[45] The five proposed areas of reform are: People, Doctrine, Partnerships, Resources, and Organization.

People

Recruit, prepare, and retain high quality personnel, including a fresh approach to the recruitment, preparation, and retention of personnel and leadership for UN peace operations.
The UN faces challenges regarding both its own staff (senior officers, planners, etc.) and those UN peacekeeping staff contributed by member states (police, military observers (MILOBS), and troops). Military capacities are of particular concern. As Under-Secretary-General Guéhenno describes it, UNDPKO urgently needs "substantial reinforcements in all functions—planning, force generation, and current operations. More military personnel are required not only to support planning of new operations and to participate in the integrated management of ongoing missions but also to help develop doctrine and guidance in the new areas of activity, a central one of which is the Joint Operations Centers and the Joint Mission Analysis Centers.[46] Police deployments have increased by 30 percent in 2006; therefore, UNDPKO is proposing the reinforcement of the Police Division and a further expansion of the Standing Police Capacity.

Accomplishments to date. In keeping with the need to recognize that peacekeeping should no longer be managed as a temporary need, the Secretary General has proposed the establishment of a 2,500-strong peacekeeping cadre of occupational groups in both the professional and field service categories. Much like the impetus behind the creation of S/CRS, the purpose of the cadre is to develop a permanent professional staff to meet today's peacekeeping needs. These personnel would meet the UN's baseline human resources requirements to support peace operations. The Secretary General also has put forward a proposal to improve recruitment processes, harmonize contractual arrangements for all staff, improve conditions of service for staff serving in the field, and offer buyout packages. A review of

---

[44] Guéhenno remarks.
[45] Statement by UN Under-Secretary-General Jean-Marie Guéhenno to the Special Committee on Peacekeeping Operations, February 26, 2007.
[46] Ibid. Under-Secretary-General Guéhenno notes that the current strategic military cell may be a valuable complement to the military component but not an alternative to a properly resourced Department.

conditions in the field is also underway. UNDPKO is seeking to make field conditions uniform for staff and to require all UN HQ staff to serve in the field. UNDPKO has also developed a program to recruit and train high caliber personnel for senior mission leadership positions, including through a policy for recruitment and a Senior Mission Leaders Course developed in 2005-6.

The Secretary General also has proposed ways to professionalize peacekeeping. DKPO has established an Integrated Training Service for military, police, and civilian training staff. A training team to be based in Brindisi, Italy, is also being recruited. New staff now receive induction training prior to deployment and new senior staff receive leadership induction training. The UN is also considering establishing additional Brindisi-type forward bases, primarily for training, in Nairobi and Addis Ababa.[47]

UN Deficiencies. The key problem regarding personnel is that UNDPKO lacks a career system for its personnel, due largely to the erroneous assumption that peacekeeping is a temporary requirement. The UN now recognizes the need for a permanent professional staff and is taking steps to acquire one but will need assistance from member states to do so. In addition, while many steps are proposed or underway, UNDPKO continues to lack up-to-date training curricula for priority operational and specialist areas, overall policy on the selection of senior mission leadership and their preparation, and review of conditions of service to promote mobility across the UN system. Training and equipping of troops is a nation's responsibility, and the UN has only limited ability to affect how nations address that challenge. Training and retention of UN personnel will require ongoing support, particularly training such personnel between deployments, a capability the UN lacks. Training and exercising of units is a particular challenge as units return to different countries once a mission is completed. Member states are often reluctant to sign up for the UN's Standby Arrangement System, largely because they perceive doing so would be making firm commitments to an unknown mission. In some cases, the reluctance may be due more to a desire to avoid revealing their actual capabilities, rather than reluctance to actually committing troops.[48]

Doctrine

Set out the doctrine, including articulating what UN peacekeeping can and cannot do and eventually set standards for UN peacekeeping missions with uniform practices and procedures.
There is agreement on the need for a doctrine of UN peacekeeping to ensure that, in the face of diverse operational environments, personnel, and mandates, a coherent body of principles and procedures to enhance safety and effectiveness guides field activities. Under the new organizational arrangement, the need for common policies, standard operating procedures, and guidance will be the basis for effective cooperation.[49] While much doctrine already exists, the key will be to ensure it is widely read, understood, and enforced.

Accomplishments to date. DPKO is beginning to issue standard peacekeeping guidance materials in four formats: policy directives, standard operating procedures, manuals, and guidelines. A first doctrinal framework has been produced, and efforts are well underway to catalogue current doctrinal holdings against this framework. A high-level doctrine publication is

---

[47] Information on the accomplishments to date in this section and the ones below are drawn from a memo to all UNDPKO staff in HQ and field from the UN Undersecretary General for Peacekeeping dated August 11, 2006 and interviews with UNDPKO staff.

[48] Discussion with UN Lessons Learned official, September 26, 2006.

[49] Guéhenno statement to the Special Committee on Peacekeeping Operations, February 26, 2007.

in the first stages of development. Policies on command and control, conduct and discipline, civil-military liaison, and a number of specialized policies and other materials are all being created. The Police Division has made great progress over the past year in putting in place doctrinal policies and procedures. Among others, policies on the establishment and employment of Joint Operation Centers (JOCs) and Joint Military Analysis Cells (JMACs) as well as procedures for crisis response for missions have been established. The first version of a DKPO intranet platform to provide guidance materials to all staff has been launched. Another version will be issued following feedback from the field missions. The UN is also developing knowledge management activities to ensure full use of the lessons learned. Further guidelines will be issued following additional feedback.

UN Deficiencies. DPKO is putting in place a comprehensive system of guidance on UN peacekeeping but lacks the resources to ensure that its doctrine development work reflects best practices, elaborates policy, and establishes standard operating procedures. Doctrine involving the use of force in missions remains problematic and unevenly interpreted, in part because the TCCs have the final say on what their troops do. The UN does not yet have a sufficiently well-resourced doctrine system that incorporates lessons learned, puts them into doctrinal publications, and makes sure the latest doctrine is incorporated into TCC training. There is also a problem of ensuring doctrine is transferred to the field missions once it is deployed. At that stage, the bulk of high-level operational and lower-end strategic planning becomes the responsibility of the head of mission in the field.[50]

Partnerships

Establish effective partnerships, including improving the integrated mission planning process, establishing clear chains of authority, and providing guidelines on "quick wins" in cooperation with UN partners. The goal is to establish frameworks for cooperation with regional organizations in peace operations, including common peacekeeping standards, joint/combined training exercises, and modalities for cooperation and transition in peace operations. This includes partnerships with regional entities, such as the EU and the Economic Community of West African States (ECOWAS), as well as newer partners like the World Bank. The restructuring of the Headquarters may also enable senior managers to devote more time to leading the strategic direction of partnerships.[51] The new AFRICOM provides an excellent opportunity for enhanced U.S.-UN partnerships as well.

Accomplishments to date. A comprehensive strategy for UNDKPO support to AU peacekeeping capacities is now in place, along with a joint UNDPKO-AU action plan. Recruitment of staff for a support unit for AU peacekeeping in Addis and New York is underway. An enhanced partnership with the EU led to the deployment of EU forces to support the UN peacekeeping mission in the Democratic Republic of Congo in the recent elections.[52] The Integrated Mission Planning Process (IMPP) to integrate all missions has been completed, and UNDPKO is piloting supporting training material.

UN Deficiencies. UNDPKO still lacks a global comprehensive system for such complex coordination or the capability to conduct such coordination. UNDPKO is upgrading its IMPP and Guidance of Integrated Missions clarifying roles. It is developing a strategy to implement the World Summit decision to establish a 10-year, capacity-building program for AU

---

[50] Email exchange with UN official September 25, 2006.
[51] Guéhenno statement to the Special Committee on Peacekeeping Operations.
[52] *Mission des Nations Unies en République Démocratique du Congo* (MONUC).

peacekeeping. Senior AU officials have expressed a desire for the UN to serve as principle coordinator for AU assistance programs, as the AU is unable to manage on its own the ongoing international efforts. Should the UN agree to take on that role, it will need assistance. No one country, let alone DOD, can address this deficiency. Rather, the Core Group could help identify needs and secure assistance.

UNDPKO needs modalities and procedures for cooperating with the EU in post-conflict situations, decisions on how best to cooperate with NATO on peacekeeping, and a framework for cooperation with the World Bank and IMF, in particular in the context of peacebuilding. There is little strategic planning with non-western countries. UNDPKO needs agreed frameworks for transitions from regional operations to UN operations. UNDKPO's next priority in the area of partnerships is to develop an approach to Security Sector Reform (SSR), and it welcomes assistance from the United States.[53] The lack of coordination has a real impact on the ground. For instance, UNDPKO officials report that EU and UN military operations during the recent disturbances in Kinshasa were less coordinated than desired, and there was no single chain of command.[54] In response, UNDPKO will create a "one-stop-shop" at HQ to provide peacekeeping operations with the strategic policies, guidance, technical advice, and information on SSR. The SSR Support Unit would be in UNDPKO and serve as a resource for the entire UN system.[55]

In Africa, partnerships can be especially helpful in building a regional hub for training and equipping. "They can get better, and bilateral relationships are the way to do it, with train and sustain assistance."[56] While ECOWAS has a small hub, a much large one would greatly enhance the sustainability and training of African forces. As the United States establishes its new AFRICOM, the placement of a UN liaison officer in AFRICOM could help facilitate a UN-U.S. partnership in Africa.

UNDPKO also lacks translation capacity in languages beyond the official UN languages. The lack of resources to translate materials into the languages of troops speaking other languages is therefore a problem.

Resources

Secure the essential resources to improve operations, including strengthening the operational capability through the establishment of a standing police capability and capacities to deploy military capabilities rapidly, strengthening the coordination and use of information technology (IT), and communicating effectively with the pubic in mission areas and home countries.

Accomplishments to date. The UN Police Division, created in October 2000, has made significant progress in creating a Standing Police Capacity (SPC) for early deployment to new missions or for assistance to ongoing missions. It also has greatly expanded the deployment of 125 member formed police units (FPUs) to the missions while actively recruiting individual officers from 86 police contributing countries.[57] The SPC will greatly enhance the ability of the UNDPKO to establish policing capacity quickly in new missions and backstop existing ones. There has been progress on rapidly deployable IT systems (with strong support from the United States). A review of the financial instruments and policy for the field is underway. As one UN

---

[53] Interview with UN official, September 14, 2006.
[54] Email exchange September 3, 2006.
[55] Guéhenno statement to the Special Committee on Peacekeeping Operations.
[56] Lute remarks.
[57] The Division was originally called UN Civilian Police (CivPol) but "Civilian" is no longer used. This progress report reflects an email exchange with a senior UNDPKO police official, October 9, 2006.

staff officer put it, "It does not make sense to make the field people use the same procedures to buy a pencil with rules established in 1950 for UN headquarter personnel."[58] A new policy on information management is now in place to get more effective information support to peacekeepers. The use of FPUs in UN peacekeeping missions has increased in recent years, with 34 approved units in six of the major UN missions worldwide.[59]

UN Deficiencies. Little progress has been made on the Military Strategic Reserve, although UNDPKO urgently needs a reserve capacity to deploy military capabilities rapidly. The United States and other member states have rejected the proposal as too costly. The UN is reviewing its UN Standby Arrangement System (UNSAS). As noted, UN officials complain that countries are reluctant to sign up for the program. The UN needs to strengthen the coordination and use of IT in the field and employ a better public information capacity in the headquarters. Finance, management, and procurement policies need to become more field oriented. Member states must pay their dues in full and on time.

Regarding police, deficiencies identified by the UN include lack of standards on basic issues, such as crowd control and management. More emphasis is needed on support for institution-building capability. The issue is less a matter of training bodies than building institutional capacity and support. At the moment, the program tends to be donor not demand driven. Additional training to "level up participants" is needed as well as "tactical help," such as security, training the force, infrastructure building, and contingency planning. UN officials indicate the need is greater than the supply and that they need a roster with a state of readiness. Some officials have suggested the United States could assist in helping to secure a commitment of 0.1 percent to 1 percent of police forces ready to deploy. UN officials also have requested assistance from DOD in coordinating police programs with other military programs, saying, "Police, justice, and counterterrorism programs are not in balance with the military."[60] Regarding FPUs, the expensive nature of the required personnel and self-sustaining equipment necessary to be fully operational has meant difficulties in fielding them.[61]

Organization

UNDPKO has three key priorities: strategic planning, the establishment of integrated teams at UN HQ and in the field, and effective business processes.

Accomplishments to date. UNDPKO is restructuring the department around a series of integrated teams that will provide staff "more effective and synthesized" support and a single point of entry for mission issues at UN HQ. An OIOS review of UNDPKO management structures is underway. Upon its completion, UNDPKO will move to establish effective business processes, including greater delegation of decisionmaking and training for headquarters staff. There are also plans to boost UNDPKO capacity to support rule of law and SSR activities. UNDKPO has made great strides in the last year in disarmament, demobilization, and reintegration (DDR) and has established an Interagency Integrated Disarmament Demobilization and Reintegration Standards (IDDRS) unit to integrate UN DDR standards. This process is led by DPKO and involves 14 UN agencies.

---

[58] Interview with UN official, September 14, 2006.

[59] Concept Paper on Equipping Formed Police Units Through Bilateral or Multilateral Arrangements, UNDPKO, February 2007. See Annex for full text.

[60] Interviews with senior police UN officials, July 28 and August 2, 2006.

[61] See Concept Paper on Equipping FPUs through Bilateral or Multilateral Arrangements, UNDPKO, February 2007 for full details of needs. Available at < http://www.ndu.edu/ctnsp/Defense_Tech_Papers.htm>.

Beyond UNDPKO, another important accomplishment has been the recent establishment of the Peacebuilding Commission (PBC) to assist nations in transition. Created to respond to gaps in existing international efforts to assist countries in making the transition from war to peace, the new body's responsibilities include advising and helping to shape coherent strategies for post-conflict transition; giving countries in transition a forum to engage with international counterparts; mobilizing resources and ensuring predictable financing; developing best practices; improving coordination; and sustaining diplomatic and donor attention to provide a solid foundation for long-term peace and development. The inaugural meeting took place June 23, 2006, and soon thereafter the 31-member body decided that Burundi and Sierra Leone would be the first two countries to receive PBC support. The PBC also includes a Peacebuilding Support Office and a Standing Fund.

Within the context of the restructuring effort, UNDPKO has proposed the establishment of an Evaluations Section staffed with civilian, military, and police personnel dedicated to self-evaluations on a more regular basis. Currently, UNDPKO has a system of evaluation in which former force commanders and other experienced senior military and police officers conduct periodic evaluations of the effectiveness of the forces. The Military Division maintains a roster of potential participants in the evaluations and has one officer dedicated part-time to the effort. The proposal will be reviewed by the General Assembly.[62] The USG has pressed for an internal UNDKPO auditor (separate from OIOS) to enhance compliance of UN Missions with UN standards, once they are articulated in doctrinal materials. UNDKPO officials indicate openness to this step.

UN Deficiencies. UNDPKO will need political support, staff, and expertise as it moves to establish effective business processes; boost its capacity to support rule of law and SSR activities; improve its overall organizational structure in the field of peacekeeping; establish integrated units, including UNDPKO Integrated Training Service and Conduct and Discipline Units; and establish integrated Operations Teams. The Evaluations Sections has yet to be established; there is no internal UNDKPO auditor. UNDPKO also faces challenges integrating the political and military functions. "The challenge is to get the relationship right between the civilian leaders and the military leaders," with clear strategic direction from the start. The UN believes the political side needs to be in the lead. Managing intelligence is also "tricky," but easier to do at the operational level under the guise of force protection.[63] While outside UNDPKO, the PBC is in its embryonic stages and needs assistance in setting priorities and developing relationships with the various UN bodies and UNDPKO activities. Specific planning and management of the peacebuilding operations also will be needed.

To accomplish these goals, the UN will need assistance from the United States and other nations with key enabling capabilities currently lacking in the UN. There are a vast number of possible areas in which DOD could assist UN peacekeeping efforts. The next two sections seek to outline those within the current political limits of the UN, Washington, and the international community and offer recommendations on a way forward.

---

[62] Email exchange with UNDPKO official, April 20, 2007.
[63] Guéhenno remarks.

Political Obstacles to the Provision of DOD Support to UNDPKO

There are significant political obstacles to DOD providing more assistance to the UN from four key areas: the Administration, UN member states, DOD, and Congress.

First, the Administration's relationship with the UN and some member states is strained, complicating progress. UN officials complain of unwarranted political attacks against the United Nations and a lack of support for much of the Secretary General's agenda. The Administration is also focused on other important priorities, especially Iraq and Afghanistan, reducing the ability of senior officials to spend time on UN issues. U.S. operations in both countries are placing a strain on the U.S. budget and limiting resources for UN peacekeeping efforts. A more constructive approach from the Administration during its second term has already begun to improve the atmosphere. The U.S. Congress, however, continues to refuse to fund UN peacekeeping operations on time and in full. Part of the problem is the lack of awareness of the vast reforms that have taken place over the last decade. A stronger Administration-wide push for full and on-time funding is essential.

Second, within the UN, many developing countries reject assistance from the United States and other developed nations, driven by concerns over their own loss of influence in the process. Perhaps the most glaring example is the 1997 ban by the General Assembly against *gratis* military officers, which prohibited the provision at no cost of military personnel from member states. The result was the departure of key military planners from a variety of NATO countries (including the United States) at the very moment peacekeeping demands were vastly increasing. Since that time, the United States has been able to secure one position in the Military Division, although it has continued to provide assistance through the military staff of USUN. Because the formal UN staff system seeks global representation and gender balance, the United States is limited in practice in how many military officers it can expect to assign to UNDPKO. Although some in the USG are under the impression that there is a limit of two positions at UN HQ, UNDPKO officials deny such a limit and continue to encourage the USG to apply for more positions.[64] Especially as UNDKPO expands its military staff and positions shift with the creation of two departments, new opportunities for UN military officers will likely arise. DOD has expressed some frustration over the UN wanting it "both ways"—wanting more support, but only if it is not visible.[65] There is broad agreement, however, on the need for the UN to ensure that U.S. military officers are placed in key positions.

The shortage of U.S. military officers in UNDPKO HQ and peacekeeping operations in the field (see table on next page) denies the UN the most capable troops in the world. Participation need not be large numbers of troops or formed units, but rather key deployments to field headquarters to assist in planning and operations. Such an increase will provide DOD valuable knowledge and expertise essential to running an international architecture and help build up a much-needed peacekeeping expertise. It will offer the UN key contacts in DOD and informal access to a broad range of DOD capabilities. Similarly, more DOD officials in UN HQ

---

[64] For instance, one UN official responded to the question of a two-person limit, it is "definitely worth trying to change in tandem with even a slight increase in contribution, on the understanding that flexibility on level/profile will be required, taking into account overall geographic balance." Email exchange with UN official, September 25, 2006.

[65] Sharp remarks.

would assist UNDPKO as well as DOD in developing such expertise. Military and civilian assets are needed.

U.S. Deployments in UN Peacekeeping Missions as of June 2006

	MILOBS*	CIVPOL**	TROOPS	TOTAL
UNOMIG (Georgia)	2			
UNMIK (Kosovo)		222		
MINUSTAH (Haiti)		47	3	
UNMIL (Liberia)	7	8	6	
UNMEE (Eritrea/Ethiopia)	5			
UNMIS (Sudan)		9		
UNMIT (East Timor)		4		
UNTSO (Middle East)			3	
U.S. Total	14	290	12	316
UN Total	2,532	9,208	70,252	81,992

* *Military Observers*
** *Civilian Police*

That said, a variety of political issues must be taken into account should DOD decide to press for more positions. Overall geographic balance and the seniority of the job play into the decision and can limit the extent and visibility of DOD assistance.[66] As one UN official put it, there is also a "broader concern that the countries providing the troops on the ground, and taking the risks, are not the same ones that decide what operations we engage in and how we fund it and how we run it. It is this disparity that is the heart of the G77 (a group of developing countries that now numbers 132 nations) concern about U.S. and other western roles."[67] Another UNDPKO official cautioned against the United States pressing too hard for staff, saying "continued pressure from member States on selection of senior personnel may work to undermine efforts to put in place a new recruitment and appointment policy for senior managers and senior management training."[68]

In addition, as noted above, much of the UN peacekeeping system is set up on the assumption that the operations will be administrative and temporary, thus undermining the need for sustaining capabilities and training.

Third, a key political problem of the UN approach to peacekeeping is the mandates of peacekeeping missions. The mandates of peacekeeping missions are often awkward compromises that tend to make robust enforcement mandates rare. Often the host nation of the mission objects to enforcement operations or the UNSC mandate is ambiguous, especially regarding the protection of civilians. Political constraints also limit the number of nationals placed on deployed contingents. Absent a radical change in the politics of the UNSC,

---

[66] As one UN official put it, "it is already a pretty big deal that the Chief of Staff of the Military Division is a U.S. citizen (as is the Police Adviser, the ASG for Mission Support, the Director for Asia and Middle East, the Chief of Civilian Personnel, and the Special Assistant to the USG). It's not only a numbers issue, but profile as well." Email exchange September 25, 2006.
[67] Email exchange with UN official August 25, 2006.
[68] Email exchange September 25, 2006.

enforcement operations will continue to be best undertaken by coalitions of the willing, preferably with a UNSC mandate but on occasion without one.

The UN's tradition of seeking to be impartial in its mandate, driven largely out of a desire not to become involved in the conflict or because of pressure from the states involved, has often led to weak responses when challenged by various militias. The Report of the Panel on UN Peace Operations, the "Brahimi Report," made clear the inability of the UN to conduct enforcement operations. For instance, the authors recognized that the UN "does not wage war. Where enforcement action is required, it has consistently been entrusted to coalitions of willing States, with the authorization of the Security Council, acting under Chapter VII of the Charter."[69] The report also noted that the "compromises required to build consensus can be made at the expense of specificity, and the resulting ambiguity can have serious consequences in the field if the mandate is then subject to varying interpretations by different elements of a peace operation, or if local actors perceive a less than complete Council commitment to peace implementation that offers encouragement to spoilers."[70] These political issues remain a challenge.

While some progress has been made in the UN's willingness to fight back if attacked, peacekeepers are ill prepared to fight a war or conduct enforcement missions. Yet, increasingly, peacekeeping requires military force. This presents a key problem, as many of the current missions are not classic ones separating warring parties but rather ones involving failed states and threats from militias. This enhanced threat, therefore, requires enhanced training that the United States is well suited to provide.

UNDPKO considers the issue of enforcement an important doctrinal issue. As one UNDPKO official put it, "UN peacekeeping is not designed and has been proven to be systemically unable to undertake effective peace enforcement or war fighting. The doctrinal dilemma for us lies in the distinction between being robustly configured (but there with the consent) to being an enforcement enterprise . . .. We distinguish between being a peace enforcement tool and being a consent-based peacekeeping tool that needs to be configured to meet robustly deterioration in consent by spoilers. But we don't seek to get good at 'enforcement'—it's not us."[71] UN officials do, however, recognize the need to be "doctrinally and operationally well positioned for operating in environments where the mission's role and mandate is challenged by spoiler elements."[72]

The 2006 mandate for the expanded UN operation in Lebanon is robust and should be the floor, not the ceiling, for broad authorities to UN peacekeeping missions. Yet, the mission is still very much at risk.[73] The expanded mission, for instance, puts additional peacekeepers into a still volatile area, with an armed militia, Hezbollah, operating without government control and committed to the destruction of Israel. It is far from clear what the UN peacekeeping forces will do should the shaky ceasefire break down, or if Hezbollah refuses to disarm or respect the

[69] A/55/305–S/2000/809 p. 10.

[70] A/55/305–S/2000/809 p.10.

[71] Email exchange, September 25, 2006. The official also pointed out that the "application of UN [peacekeeping] to warfighting scenarios would lower the value of the tool as it currently stands—a consent-based, post-conflict stabilization tool."

[72] Email exchange with UN official, September 25, 2006.

[73] The August 11, 2006, resolution includes a strong mandate authorizing the mission to take all necessary action to ensure its area of operation is not used for hostile activities, to resist any forceful attempts to prevent it from discharging its duties, to protect UN personnel and facilities, and to protect civilians under imminent threat of physical violence. See S/Res/1701/2006 at < http://daccess-ods.un.org/access.nsf/Get?Open&DS=S/RES/1701%20(2006)&Lang=E&Area=UNDOC>.

authority of the Lebanese security forces. Political objections to the participation of certain states, not to mention the reluctance of states to volunteer for the dangerous mission, all underscore the continuing challenges of UN peacekeeping.

The strengthened peacekeeping mission in Lebanon also demonstrates a lack of faith in the UN's ability to manage and plan for complex missions. The price of EU participation in Lebanon was the establishment of a 25-person military planning staff at UN Headquarters (UN HQ) under the direction of an Italian Lieutenant General. Some at UNDPKO are concerned this step will "render the Military Division of DPKO as less or not relevant in the planning process. The reaction of non-EU/western countries to this also remains to be seen. A further implication is that this could set a precedent for future operations with the EU and, possibly, other regional organizations."[74] Given the limitations of the UN, however, such a strategic/military cell may be a model for other complex missions.

These constraints mean that peacekeeping will remain an awkward compromise among the TCCs, host nations, and UNSC members. While Pentagon assistance in helping to shape the doctrines involved can help, policymakers must understand that many of the challenges faced today by peacekeepers are a result of member states' political sensitivities and not deficiencies of UNDPKO.

For DOD, it is important that nations scale back on national caveats and include the more forceful "all necessary means" language in its mandates. Otherwise, some will take advantage of a weak mandate, putting forces at risk.[75] That said, it is important to be clear that the UN cannot be effective if there is no peace to keep. As Under-Secretary-General Guéhenno emphasizes, "It is important to be clear about what a peacekeeping operation can and cannot achieve."[76]

A particular challenge is that among the UN member states, the Non-aligned Movement (NAM), with 118 members, and the G77, with 132 members, often block U.S. reform efforts. Much of the NAM's actions are simply done in opposition to the United States. Many of these developing nations seek to block UN reform out of concern that the UN might next press for reforms in their own nations. For instance, many blocked effective reform of the Human Rights Committee and refuse to grant the UN Secretary General more power to manage the UN bureaucracy more effectively. There is also growing resentment that developing countries make up the bulk of the TCCs and that the UN is becoming a system where the rich pay and the poor deploy. As developed countries dominate the UNSC, many TCCs feel they lack sufficient say in the mandates of the peacekeeping missions in which their troops are deployed. Many member states resist direct offers of assistance from developed member states, especially the United States. For instance, when the United States offered publicly to draft the plan for a UN peacekeeping mission in Sudan, the proposal was immediately considered "dead on arrival."[77]

While more contingency planning is needed, such planning is controversial among some member states. Without an explicit authorization from the UNSC, such planning risks drawing objections from states that may claim the Secretariat has overstepped its authority and that such planning could influence the internal affairs of sovereign states. Therefore, any contingency planning would need to be on an informal, "under the radar," manner.[78]

---

[74] Email exchange with UNDPKO official, September 3, 2006.
[75] Sharp remarks.
[76] Guéhenno remarks.
[77] Interview with senior UN DPKO official, June 6, 2006.
[78] Email exchange with UN military planner, August 11, 2006.

Fourth, opposition remains strong in the USG and in Congress to the deployment of U.S. troops to UN missions for any length of time or in significant levels. Such lack of participation denies the UN key capacities and access to DOD resources and military-to-military relationships. As one UN official put it, "Merely having the U.S. [contribute] MILOBS [military observers] and staff officers creates all sorts of capacity access." American abstention, on the other hand, can discourage other nations from contributing to UN peacekeeping missions. As another UN official put it, "U.S. disinterest feeds into a reluctance of the rest. If the U.S. isn't going, others won't."[79] Domestic political pressure to limit U.S. direct involvement will remain a factor in any decision to provide support for the foreseeable future, but U.S. coordination and encouragement can be an important source of support. In Africa, for instance, European Command (EUCOM) officials found that "with coordinated support and encouragement from the U.S., allied donor nations, including NGOs [non-governmental organizations] and international corporations, Economic Community of West African States (ECOWAS) has measurably improved its capacity to respond to regionally supported operations."[80]

The scandals that have arisen from some UN peacekeeping missions—most infamously sexual exploitation— may exacerbate the reluctance of DOD to deploy personnel to UN missions. UNDPKO has made important strides in addressing misconduct, but more progress on improving controls and better investigatory procedures might alleviate some concerns.[81] In addition, concerns about putting U.S. soldiers under UN command and control, including wearing the uniforms, being paid by the UN, and taking the UN oath all remain obstacles to additional U.S. participation in the UN HQ and in field missions.

DOD also must make UN postings career-enhancing steps. Unfortunately, as one U.S. military official said, "assignment to the UN is deadly to careers."[82] DOD must ensure that it is seem as enhancing promotion prospects. Follow-on assignments to the Joint Staff and combatant commands can build much-needed DOD expertise on UN peacekeeping as well as regional expertise in some of the most troubled areas.

A related issue is the strong opposition in the USG, in Congress, and in other nations to the UN proposal to establish a strategic reserve. The UN argues that such a reserve is a necessary deterrent, as "spoilers know that what they see on the ground is what there is."[83] Member states are very reluctant to give the UN the pre-authorization to deploy forces. Any such force would need to be authorized by the General Assembly and would be an added cost to member states. While some suggest that the UN can simply add forces if a new situation arises, as NATO did in Afghanistan, the UN procedures are more cumbersome. Under-Secretary-General Guéhenno has suggested that one way to proceed would be to strengthen the standby system, with procedures and the financial arrangements in place for a possible deployment. He suggested that the most likely way forward for now is for one of the countries already in theater to step up to the commitment.[84]

Fifth, the lack of timely and flexible funding continues to impede effective peacekeeping operations. Many in Congress oppose funding to the UN and impose unrealistic conditions for reform. Some also oppose the deployment of U.S. military personnel to UN peacekeeping

---

[79] Interview with senior UN officials, June 16, 2006.
[80] Op cit., Jones, 18-19.
[81] Interview with senior UN official, September 6, 2006.
[82] Email exchange, September 11, 2006.
[83] Guéhenno remarks.
[84] Ibid.

missions, especially to countries that have not specifically exempted U.S. military officials from the International Criminal Court. DOD strongly resists any role in pressing Congress for UN funding, citing other much higher priorities.

These political realities are unlikely to change soon and must be recognized as a real hindrance to effective peacekeeping. The recommendations below take these limits into consideration and offer some suggestions on how to overcome some of these obstacles.

Recommendations for DOD Assistance to UNDPKO

Before turning to the four areas of DOD expertise specified by the QDR, it should be noted that there are five broad steps DOD should take to further assist UNDPKO that would greatly enhance the strengths, appropriateness, and efficiency of support, limit the drain on DOD resources, and assist in achieving the recommendations below.

First, the USG should develop and support a new coordination mechanism: a coalition of states a "Core Group of Support to Peace Operations" (the Core Group) to press for UNDPKO reform and coordinated assistance. Some combination of the P-5, TCC (and potential future ones), key regional organizations (AU, NATO, EU, SHIRBRIG), and the International Association of Peace Training Centers should be included. While the U.S. tends to be everyone's first port of call, other developed nations are often sufficiently capable of providing key assistance to the UN. With strong U.S. leadership, the group should help create a central database and tracking system to manage incoming offers of financial, material, and personnel support as well as training of troops. Getting others to be more responsive to UN requests will ease that burden on the United States. As part of this effort, the Core Group would respond to UNDPKO requests in a systematic way, with the United States taking on some tasks while pressing other nations to take on others. Assistance to military forces in Africa through the African Union, using the new AFRICOM as a focus, could perhaps serve as an initial focus of the group.

Second, DOD should selectively increase U.S. participation in the UN command structure. Recognizing the military needs of the UN are expanding, UNDPKO intends to increase its military positions, thereby facilitating the placement of more U.S. personnel in the department. Also, the more resources the United States provides to the UN, the easier it is to second more officers. At UNDPKO HQ in New York, DOD should press for an increase in the number of seconded billets, mainly as military planners but also more broadly to assist the UN (and DOD) develop expertise. In the field, DOD should provide more personnel to strategic headquarter positions, administrative positions, specialized enabling skills, police missions, and observation roles. While DOD believes it can succeed in securing at most two military staff positions at UN HQ, UN officials indicate more might be possible. UNDPKO must ensure any such staff is placed in value-added positions.

Third, the United States and the UN should explore additional ways to include UN officials and peacekeeping troops in ongoing activities, especially U.S. training exercises and lessons-learned efforts. While DOD is already active in many regional organizations, it should consider more active engagement in African, Latin American, and Asian organizations to help achieve and coordinate an international architecture to support peacekeeping.[85] Deployment of DOD military officers and civilian personnel to UN and regional training centers also should be considered, as they would serve as important multipliers.[86] New opportunities for partnerships, such as AFRICOM and the new National Security University, should be fully explored.

---

[85] For instance, EUCOM has an officer currently deployed to The Kofi Annan International Peacekeeping Training Centre (KAIPTC) in Accra, Ghana.

[86] The five DOD Centers for Regional Security, international regional peacekeeping centers, and regional organizations can provide useful educational centers and training opportunities on the challenges of peacekeeping. They could serve as useful multipliers of promoting doctrine, training, and other support to UNDKPO.

Trilateral dialogues with the United States, UN, and key potential African partners should be considered. A UN liaison to AFRICOM should be considered.

Fourth, the United States and the UN should press for formal inclusion of UN peacekeeping in the agendas of the G-8 summit meetings. Given the importance of peacekeeping in meeting today's threats, as well as the wide variety of needs, the issue must be addressed at the highest levels of those with the most to offer.

Fifth, there needs to be more consistent, high-level dialogue on UN needs and how to meet them. One option to achieve that goal would be annual or semi- annual offsite senior-level strategic dialogues, such as the one hosted by the National Defense University (NDU) on March 2, 2007. NDU stands ready to host more such meetings, and the UN has indicated a willingness to participate.[87] A regular UN "wish-list" for USG consideration might also be helpful.

The following are more specific recommendations for the short and longer term, primarily for DOD but also for overall USG policy toward UNDPKO.

Short-Term Areas for Greater DOD Assistance

The QDR identified four areas of potential support—strategic planning, doctrine, management, and training—which are analyzed immediately below, followed by discussions of police, five longer-term issues, and four areas for additional consideration. This report adds a fifth, the police. Recognizing the demands placed on DOD by the GWOT and operations in Afghanistan and Iraq, these recommendations call for limited DOD participation with the expectation that other forces will be encouraged to do more. Another benefit of participation is that the experience gained will enable DOD to better conduct stability operations pursuant to Directive 3000.05.

Strategic planning. Overall, UN officials believe UN strategic planning doctrine is not centralized enough, with too much responsibility in the field, in contrast with NATO's, which is perhaps too centralized. UNDPKO would welcome assistance in further developing planning doctrine at the strategic versus field/theatre level.

Contrary to the conventional wisdom that the UN plans poorly for its missions, it actually has learned how to do so well. Joint Staff officials concur in that view. The UN has learned from the failures of peacekeeping in the 1990s. It has the capability to plan for major missions, with 64 people in its military division, including 43 military officers, 12 of whom are military planners, many from NATO countries. With over 100,000 personnel in the field in 20 peace missions, the UN HQ is in fact quite efficient in its planning. Contrasted with the 1600 planners assigned to NATO, some question whether more are even needed at the UN. But as one UN official put it, "we do not have to plan for all the contingencies NATO plans for." NATO, in fact, offered to help with UN planning but the UN does not feel it needs such assistance.[88] No UN official interviewed identified planning for specific missions as a deficiency. They did say that when rapid planning is necessary, a surge planning capacity is needed and UNDPKO officials would welcome DOD assistance in that regard.

Recommendation. Make DOD military planners available on an *ad hoc* and temporary basis to address the surge capacity need, mostly through USUN. These activities should be kept low profile to avoid potential backlash from other member states. DOD could provide personnel

---

[87] In his remarks, UN Under-Secretary-General Guéhenno indicated he was open to participating in future meetings and expressed an interest in issues such as AFRICOM and Provincial Reconstruction Teams (PRTs). DOD indicated it could use "better take-aways" on exactly what the UN needs.

[88] Interview with UN official June 6, 2006.

to assist on lessons learned and doctrine at UN HQ, as well as assist in the field with integrated planning. Civilian assistance should be included, as well as personnel with expertise in technology, finance, and procurement areas. Developing ways to make lessons learned more actionable and more quickly implemented, as well as a U.S.–UN sharing mechanism, would be useful.

Another complaint from the UN is that it is often pushed to plan hurriedly during a crisis. As one UNDPKO Official explained, "We are forced to operate in ways not even a modestly competent government would accept. In Darfur, we were asked to assess a $1 billion operation in only two weeks. Even a moderately organized government would reserve the right to move in two to eight months. We want 'froid planning, not chaud," meaning the UN is often pressed to plan in the middle of a crisis, not the cooler-headed environment of non-crisis planning.[89]

Recommendation. The United States could assist the UN in long-term contingency planning along the lines NATO currently does. Exercises could be conducted on an annual or semi-annual basis and involve general doctrine and best practices training. Such support would help UNDPKO develop options to use in pre-selecting its planning options. Such assistance could be done by DOD, through the peacekeeping institutes, or in concert with NATO, the EU, and/or other regional organizations.

Recommendation. The intelligence community should develop a system of intelligence sharing that could assist the UN in immediate tactical needs, as well as information on possible longer-term future conflicts to assist the UN in contingency planning. Doing so at the operational level as part of force protection might ease some of the political difficulties involved.

When asked about the need for strategic planning, UN officials repeatedly mention the need for better intelligence, both tactical to know what is happening in the field and strategic to be able to plan over the horizon. In discussions in June 2006 with UN officials, for instance, a number of them emphasized how helpful it would be to have information on the activities of the militia in the DRC or the Lord's Resistance Army (LRA) in Uganda. Cell phone tracking and tactical surveillance could be of enormous assistance to the UN. Cartographic information also would be of great assistance to the UN's Global Information System. In addition, senior UN officials expressed a desire for strategic briefings on current and future potential conflicts. From 1998-2001, the National Intelligence Council (NIC) conducted high-level briefings of such conflicts to senior UN officials and representatives of the UNSC. The practice appears to have been lost in the transition between administrations in 2001.

Recommendation. As AFRICOM is established, first in Stuttgart, Germany and then in Africa by October 2008, the United States and UN should establish ways to assist the AU develop its peacekeeping capabilities. The European nations, either through the EU or NATO, should take on lead roles. S/CRS also may have a unique contribution to the effort, especially given its recent experience with placing representatives at the various COCOMs. Placing a UN liaison in AFRICOM should be considered. The Core Group could help coordinate the effort.

Doctrine. UNDPKO lacks uniform practices and procedures as well as training standards for UN peacekeeping missions. It also lacks a comprehensive system of guidance that reflects best practices, elaborates policy, and establishes standard operating procedures. The need is particularly acute in SSR and police development, as well as procedures in situations where the use of force may be required. Progress has been made in DDR but further assistance is needed. While DOD does not have the lead on either SSR or police, it can still assist in the

---

[89] Interview with senior UN official June 6, 2006.

efforts. The fundamentals continue to evolve and the UN welcomes continued assistance in the application and limits of peacekeeping.[90]

Recommendation. DOD should continue to develop and share with UNDPKO peacekeeping guidance framework in the areas identified by UNDPKO: policy directives, standard operating procedures, manuals, and guidelines. The UN is keen on participating in exercises to build doctrine at the operational and strategic levels, as well as horizontal links, such as between the police and military. The UN also needs assistance in coordinating and implementing such standards with contributing nations.

Behind the scenes, DOD could also help promote standardized international peacekeeping doctrine through the various regional peacekeeping centers.[91] For instance, the U.S. Army Peacekeeping and Stability Operations Institute (PKSOI) is already assisting with UNDPKO doctrine development efforts, including potentially taking a leading responsibility for them. Other such centers could provide key assistance. PKSOI and other centers should also consider a role in developing, distributing, and teaching a standard international peacekeeping doctrine for use by TCCs. Should the new National Security University become a reality, it would provide a good opportunity for the United States to work with the UN and other partners in the future.

The United States and the UN should find a mechanism to share the lessons learned in real time; one effective option is to place small teams on the ground with missions. The experiences of the USG with Provisional Reconstruction Teams (PRTs) in Iraq and Afghanistan could also provide useful lessons learned and doctrine.

Annual meetings among key players in UNDPKO, DOS, DOD, and regional organizations should be initiated to assist in developing and implementing doctrine. Involvement of the Core Group recommended above should be central to the effort. As UNDPKO turns to SSR, DOD could assist in the development of its doctrine in that area, as well as provide managers and trainers to the effort.

DOD could assist in the translation of material to TCCs not speaking the UN languages. DOD also could work to ensure that troops trained by the United States (whether throughthe various DOS or DOD programs) are trained in UN doctrine so they are aware of UN procedures and standards should they be deployed at a later stage to UN missions.

Management. UNDPKO needs assistance in selecting and retaining senior mission personnel; maintaining a roster of capable troops; finding ways to promote mobility across the UN system; establishing integrated organizational structures at UN HQ and in the field; and incorporating political, military, police, specialist civilian, logistics, financial, personnel, and public information support expertise. UNDPKO also could use advice in its overall organizational structure in the field of peacekeeping, establishing integrated units, including UNDPKO Integrated Training Service and Conduct and Discipline Unit and integrated Operations Teams.

Recommendation. DOD can advise UNDPKO on developing these management improvements. Overall, an interagency working group should be established to assist the UN in each of its five tasks and to work closely with the UNDPKO cross-disciplinary Task Force and working groups in each of the five areas identified as priorities by the UN identified in the first

---

[90] Guéhenno remarks.
[91] UNDPKO officials caution against too visible a role. "We do not want a sense that we are cooking up international standards or the intergovernmental process will jump all over it, requiring intensive negotiations which will probably smother it." Email exchange February 27, 2007

section above. DOD also can continue to press for an internal DKPO auditor (separate OIOS) to enhance compliance of UN Missions with UN standards, once they are articulated in doctrinal materials. UNDKPO officials indicate openness to this step.[92] Such a step would be useful in addition to the establishment of the Evaluations Section by the General Assembly.

Training. UNDPKO needs assistance in the areas of enabling capabilities, doctrine, management, retention of personnel, IT, finance and procurement policies, public information, and ways to sustain forces. Specialized technical skills such as logistics and communications are especially important. Senior UNDPKO officials point to the integrated missions as a model. U.S. officials believe the PRTs in Afghanistan and Iraq offer good models. Regarding AFRICOM, they emphasize that this new command center will offer the ability to have U.S. forces in the field interact with UN country missions without having to go back to UN headquarters "for everything."[93]

Recommendation. DOD should provide a variety of training and encourage others, especially the Europeans, either through the EU or NATO, to take responsibility for certain areas. Bilateral relationships are the most effective way to train and equip. Areas to be considered include integrated training services, up-to-date training curricula for priority operational and specialist areas, and ongoing support and training of such personnel in between deployments to assist in the retention of personnel. One high priority area is force protection training for UN forces, especially as the risk to peacekeepers is growing.[94]

The UN needs to strengthen the coordination and use of IT capacities in the field, particularly in support of JOC/JMAC.[95] It also needs a better public information capacity in the UN HQ and to facilitate better communications among field commanders. Finance and procurement policies need reform and DOD could assist in these areas. Achieving sustainability will be key. A bottom-up approach to training and equipping should also be considered as, currently, the Ambassadors ask piecemeal for assistance.[96]

One of the key problems of the training of peacekeeping troops is the failure to sustain the battalions. DOS has the lead responsibility for training African peacekeeping forces through its Global Peace Operations Initiative (GPOI). Its goal is to train 75,000 troops by 2009, two-thirds of which will be in Africa.[97] The G-8 has also endorsed this goal. Yet, achieving any level of sustainability will require vastly more ambitious training and equipping programs. DOD, working with the Core Group could help achieve that goal. Possible areas to assist include annual training exercises, work plans, and assistance in transition from military to civilian participants.[98] An African training hub also would be useful. DOD also could consider assisting in pre-deployment orientation and training for U.S. and international military and civilian personnel

---

[92] For instance, as one UNDKPO senior official put it, "there must be a General audit and oversight function here in the organization (like GAO), but each operating dept should also have an IG (like each agency in the U.S. government has one (DOD, State, the Army, etc)." Email exchange September 26, 2006.

[93] Comment of Lute, NDU offsite, March 2, 2007.

[94] Ibid.

[95] Joint Operations Center (for crisis response) and Joint Mission Analysis Cell.

[96] Comment of Col. Scott Moore, Director of Strategic Initiatives (Partnership Strategies) at DOD, NDU offsite, March 2, 2007.

[97] GPOI's FY06 budget was $114 million, although Congress only funded it at $100 million. The FY07 request is $102 million. The United States provides training and equipment and assists African troops in the key enablers of deployment, troop sustainment, air traffic control, electricians, etc.

[98] Testimony by Victoria K. Holt, The Henry L. Stimson Center, Hearing on "African Organizations and Institutions: Positive Cross-Continental Progress," Subcommittee on African Affairs, Senate Foreign Relations Committee, November 17, 2005.

assigned to long-term missions. It must be recognized that a major problem is also the high turnover rates among the peacekeeping troops. UNDPKO also suggests DOD could support the development of senior training programs, including senior training modules (STM) and senior leadership induction programs (SLIP).[99]

In addition to specific ongoing training, DOD should consider broader, more international use of the peacekeeping training efforts already underway, such as those of the Joint Readiness Training Center at Fort Polk, Louisiana. PKSOI and other regional peacekeeping centers should play a stronger role in such training, including UNDKPO personnel and TCC troops. DOD should direct that PKSOI, in conjunction with other regional training centers, participate in the development of annual exercises for UNDKPO personnel and TCC troops. Such training efforts should be coordinated through the above-recommended Core Group.

Police. While the International Criminal Investigative Training Assistance Program (ICITAP) is located in DOS, there are areas in policing in which DOD could provide assistance to UNDPKO. While UN officials caution that the U.S. military is not trained for the type of interaction with civilian populations most UN missions involve, they believe there are still areas in which DOD could assist the UN. Deficiencies identified by the UN include lack of standards on basic issues, such as crowd control and management. At the moment, the program tends to be donor not demand driven. Additional training to "level up participants" is needed, as well as "tactical help," such as security, training the force, infrastructure building, and contingency planning. UN officials indicate the need is greater than the supply and that there is a need for a roster with a state of readiness. Some officials have suggested the United States could assist in helping to secure a commitment of .1 percent to 1 percent of police forces ready to deploy. UN officials also suggested assistance from DOD in coordinating police programs with other military programs, saying, "The police, justice, counterterrorism, and other programs are not in balance with the military."[100] The UN concept of operations calls for 16 FPUs with 125 members in each. The USG could assist the UN in reaching that goal, perhaps through the G-8 and Core Group.

Officials complain about the lack of police advisors in the Permanent Missions of member states (most have military advisors). Currently, police advisors are in only seven Permanent Missions: Sweden, Nigeria, France, Australia, Spain, Argentina, and Cameroon. The USUN Military advisors are well respected and assist where they can, but "they are not police officers."[101]

Recommendation. As demands on police functions in peacekeeping operations expand, UNDPKO will require additional assistance in the Police Division and in expanding the Standing Police Capacity. The UN has increased significantly the use of FPUs in UN peacekeeping missions. To be fully operational, such units must have adequate and appropriate personal, collective police equipment, and self-sustaining capabilities. As police are primarily a civilian function, DOS has the primary responsibility for assisting UNDPKO Police Division. However, DOD also has capabilities of potential use to the UN, such as crowd control, basic training, infrastructure building, and contingency planning. DOS and DOD also could assist in maintaining a roster for police with a state of readiness as well as effective standby arrangements with rosters of individuals and functions. Assistance also could be provided in overall police training, coordination, and doctrine development. The USG also should consider inviting UN

---

[99] Email exchange with UNDPKO official, February 27, 2007.
[100] Interview with senior police UN official, August 2, 2006.
[101] Ibid.

trainers to join U.S. training sessions on law and order techniques, including on-line training. Placing police advisors at USUN might also be considered.

Longer-Term Issues to Be Resolved

Equipment. UN officials have repeatedly asked that troop contributors leave equipment behind for the UN operations. Doing so presents the United States a particular problem because of Congressional prohibitions on such a practice. Securing new legislation revoking such prohibitions would be difficult. One option suggested by a UN official is to review whether the current excess property program could be expanded to enable such property to be donated to the UN logistics base at Brindisi, Italy.[102] DOS authorizers consider such action equivalent to foreign assistance and oppose providing DOD any such authorities. However, a reasonable compromise should be found to enable DOD to leave equipment behind. ECOWAS in West Africa does maintain a small hub for equipment that could perhaps be expanded.

Recommendation. DOD should evaluate whether to seek a change in authorities to enable it to leave key equipment behind to the recipients of peacekeeping exercises. Ways to address DOS foreign policy concerns over excess items must be found. The. United States and UN should press the Europeans to do more, including tapping into Cold War stocks, either through the EU or NATO. A more significant Brindisi-type stockpile facility in West Africa also should be established.

Funding problems. There is no way around the need to fix the funding of UN peacekeeping if it is to meet current and future challenges. Studies abound on how to do it; it is the political will that is lacking. The Administration across the board must make a stronger case for full and on-time funding. DOD is strongly opposed to joining in that effort because of other funding priorities. Congress must fully fund its UN assessed dues and do so on time. It is time Congress looked at peacekeeping as central to GWOT. As noted, those efforts specified in the Roadmap include the capability to defeat terrorist networks, shape the choices of countries at strategic crossroads, prevent hostile states and non-state actors from acquiring or using WMD, conduct SSTR operations, and enable host countries to provide good governance.[103]

One option that has been suggested in UN circles, including by the Secretary General's High Level Panel, is for peacekeeping operations undertaken by regional organizations but endorsed by the UNSC to be funded by assessed contributions.[104] For instance, the AU operation in Darfur has faced numerous funding difficulties. Assessed contributions for the limited number of regional deployments blessed by the UNSC would assist the UN, which usually ends up taking over the missions.[105]

Recommendation. The failure to reimburse troop contributors and continued failure of the United States to pay its UN assessments on time and in full undermines UN peacekeeping efforts. The USG must make funding a priority, stressing the UN role in GWOT and making it clear that the UN is a central part of the post-9/11 war on terrorism. All UNSC-blessed peacekeeping missions, including regional ones, should be funded by assessed contributions.

Rapid Deployment Reserves. While the politics of the issue in Washington are difficult ("dead on arrival" is the most common description), UNDPKO continues to press for a

---

[102] Email exchange with UN military planner, August 11, 2006.

[103] QDR Executive Roadmap, section 1.3.3.

[104] For more information, see the High-level Panel on Threats, Challenges, and Change's report, *A More Secure World: Our Shared Responsibility* <http://www.un.org/secureworld/report3.pdf>.

[105] The UN's High-level panel recommended such operations be assessed as well.

reserve capacity to deploy military capabilities rapidly. The UN argues such a step is only prudent, especially as attackers know there is no back up. The idea remains very controversial in the USG, in Congress, and with other potential contributors. Any such reserve would need to be funded through the General Assembly. The USG should discuss the needs of the UN in this regard and explore options. While it is difficult for DOD to put its own forces on reserve, more could be done to press other nations to do so. Support for any proposals will need to be secured in a skeptical Congress. On enhanced, rapidly deployable capacities, UNDPKO is exploring a range of options, including inter-mission cooperation, regional cooperation in support of UN operations, and TCC participation, possibly through premium-level reimbursements.[106]

Recommendation. Given the myriad threats to UN forces, the idea deserves further discussion and study, perhaps including support for the concept, with others providing the capacity. The UN hopes countries, especially those already deployed in an operation, will agree to provide certain capacities within a certain timeframe, with pre-agreed financial arrangements. One possible starting point for discussion is UNDKPO's suggestion that DOD support efforts to revise its UN Standby Arrangement Systems and use the Core Group to promote sign up by countries concerned. It is important to remember that sign up does not entail automatic deployment. The model used in the Congo in which additional troops were inserted to address a specific situation may be useful.

Enabling capacities. One of the key deficiencies in troops made available to UN peacekeeping missions (and AU operations most acutely) is the lack of enabling capabilities, such as lift, logistics, communications, medical units, electronics, and basic troop sustainment (one deficiency that keeps the costs of the operations much lower). Given the U.S. history of fighting wars in distant lands, no nation is better equipped to assist others in developing such capabilities. Expanding logistics hubs to locations beyond Brindisi should be considered.

Recommendation. DOD could provide some enabling capacities and seek lead nations to provide assistance in remaining areas. It should seek key hubs for support to UN missions and regional forces, especially in Africa. Again, such efforts should be coordinated through a Core Group and the issue of who covers the costs would need to be resolved.

Expanding and strengthening UN certified programs. Standard training for civilian, military, and police personnel in UN operations is difficult because member states—not the UN--have the responsibility for training their personnel. Member states' commitment to training varies. But UNDPKO has a good system of UN certification for police and military troops, and regularly visits potential participants to determine their suitability for deployment. UNDPKO's Standard Generic Training Modules (STGM) and Standardized Training Modules (STM) provide good standards. The certification process involves UN assessing the capability of national or regional training centers to meet these UN standards. Nearly all TCC incorporate or conform to the UN STGM/STM system as part of pre-deployment training.

Recommendation. Continue working with partner organizations (Challenges, Conference of American Armies, International Association of Peace Training Centers, G-8 Global Peacekeeping Operations Initiative) and allies to encourage the expanded use of standard training. Training teams could then work with the regional organizations and various national and regional peacekeeping training centers to provide this standard training. DOD could assist in the development of modules and help spread the acceptance of and compliance with the standards. Promoting these standards through the regional peacekeeping missions also should be

---

[106] Email exchange with UNDKPO Official, February 27, 2007.

considered. Invitations to key peacekeeping officials at the UN and in regional organizations to participate in U.S. War Colleges and other educational opportunities should be considered.

Areas for Further Study

U.S. and international efforts to assist in UN peacekeeping are extensive. But there is no overall strategic plan to coordinate their efforts within USG agencies or among international efforts. In addition, there is essentially a firewall between peacekeeping and anti-terrorist efforts, although, while very different, there are obvious overlapping goals. There is no clear division of responsibility between DOS and DOD in the effort to build capable peacekeeping or counter-terrorism forces abroad. In addition, the communications between DOD and DOS on the issue could be improved.

It is time to undertake a bottom-up-review of how the U.S. government conducts peacekeeping support and rationalize its current approach. Such an effort would result in significant benefits to UNDPKO, which suffers from the current lack of U.S. and international coordination and failure to support fully the UN's needs. The following recommendations involve broad bottom-up-type strategic reviews and reorganizations, as well as several leadership roles for the United States.

Conduct a Comprehensive Review.

While PKSOI has a good grasp of the international efforts, a comprehensive interagency review of current U.S. support to international peacekeeping would help the USG determine what works, what does not work, and what is missing. NSPD 44 explicitly tasked DOS "to coordinate and strengthen efforts of the United States Government to prepare, plan for, and conduct reconstruction and stabilization assistance …. The relevant situations include complex emergencies and transitions, failing states, failed states, and environments across the spectrum of conflict, particularly those involving transitions from peacekeeping and other military interventions." Yet, DOD has many programs that involve exactly these roles. Such an interagency review will be crucial in determining the best way forward. The PCC might be the best group to conduct such a comprehensive, government-wide review.

Rationalize and coordinate peacekeeping and terrorism functions, including training and equipping efforts.

Over the years, separate programs to support peacekeeping operations and terrorism efforts have developed. There needs to be a more rational division of labor between DOS and DOD responsibilities. The current activities do not reflect the authorities laid out in NSPD 44. Although the programs are very different, there are synergies between them that ought to be better coordinated to ensure maximum reinforcements and efficiencies. Ultimately, an interagency decision on a division of roles between DOS and DOD is needed.

In addition, to implement fully NSPD 44, the interagency process must decide if the authorities under Sections 1206 and 1207 of the National Defense Authorization Act will be permanent. Section 1206 enables DOD to fund antiterrorism programs within DOS Department jurisdiction, such as state capacity building programs related to counterterrorism or stability operations in which the United States is a participant. Section 1207 provides DOD the authority to transfer DOD articles, services, and training to DOS to help restore or maintain peace in a country. While these programs meet an immediate need, they blur the two Department's authorities. A clear decision between the Administration and Congress on what DOS and DOD roles should be in the programs is urgently needed. Once those authorities are established, they should be generously funded—whether at DOS or DOD.

In addition, USAID has broad authorities in peacekeeping-related activities, such as support for civil society, rule of law, disarmament, and reintegration programs. The division of labor between these post-conflict programs and the role of S/CRS remains unclear and a source of bureaucratic tensions.

Coordination of DOS and DOD efforts in the field is also crucial. For instance, DOD demonstrations of force during volatile moments in a country can lend important support and credibility to peacekeeping missions.[107] More coordination with development goals is needed. For instance, UN officials site the lack of coordination in the field of peacekeeping efforts and development work as a problem. They point to the good coordination by the UK's defense and development agencies in its efforts in Sierra Leone as an example of how it should work.[108]

Help support coordinated worldwide peacekeeping improvements, especially in Africa.

Take the lead in pressing for partnerships to support the Africa Action Plan and the African Standby Force. While the United States tends to be the first port of call for UN requests, other developed nations in Europe, Latin America, and Asia are perfectly capable of meeting such requests. While NATO is focused on Afghanistan, select countries could nevertheless assist directly in aiding African forces. The UN also will also be key. The new AFRICOM provides an excellent opportunity to integrate U.S and UN efforts in Africa, as well as to press for Europeans to do more to help African peacekeepers. U.S. support to regional organizations in developing their capacities is especially welcome by the UN, including Africa, Latin America, and Asia. One key goal would be to build a permanent strategic headquarters or secretariat within the regional and/or sub-regional organizations that could support peacekeeping operations, particularly in doctrines and procedures. Each could promote a set of guidelines regarding fundamental principles, practices, and procedures.[109] The most acute need is in Africa. Seventy-five percent of UN peacekeeping missions are in Africa, although the region lacks sufficient peacekeeping capabilities to address the myriad conflicts in the continent. Roles to consider include NATO taking on a more active role and the United States assuming the lead role in the G-8 African Action Plan. Part of such an effort could include increasing GPOI significantly. It is important to recognize that absent such a broad U.S. role, the ambitious plans of the international community will most likely not be realized, including the G-8 Africa Action Plan to train and equip 75,000 troops by 2010. The AU plan to establish standby brigades in each of its five regions, totally nearly 20,000, will certainly not be reached by 2010, without substantial U.S. help. Examples of how the USG could help include:

- Help coordinate U.S. UN, NATO, EU, and regional efforts to train and equip troops to identify needs, ensure needs are met, duplication is avoided, and the right troops are

---

[107] One example cited by a UN official is the UK demonstrations of force off the coast of Freetown. They "helped bolster the credibility of the peacekeeping mission in Sierra Leone." Email exchange with UN planner August 11, 2006.

[108] As one UN official put it in an email September 25, 2006, "Development agencies often still rail against support for the political and security objectives of peace ops. Reconstruction programmers often do not form part of the political centre of gravity of the international community effort."

[109] See The Challenges Project, *Meeting the Challenges of Peace Operations: Cooperation and Coordination*, Phase II Concluding Report 2003-2006, Elanders Gotab, 2005. Available at <www.challengesproject.net>.

trained. Efforts beyond the Western powers should be included, particularly those of Asia and Latin America. The new AFRICOM will be central to this effort.

- Work with S/CRS and the Director of National Intelligence (DNI) to support data collection and analysis of capable troops, including those with niche capabilities. Such a database would include contractors.
- Expand peacekeeping exercises to include foreign troops and UN staff, especially as a way of maintaining units targeted for U.S. support.
- Offer peacekeeping procedures and doctrine on a global basis.
- Help in pre-deployment orientation and training for U.S. and international military and civilian personnel assigned to long-term missions.
- With DOS, press specific nations to take on certain lead roles for support to peacekeeping missions, such as hubs for airlift, communications, and logistical support (much as Brindisi, Italy serves as a global presupply base). Countries beyond the G-8, particularly those in Asia and Latin America, should be asked to join the effort. The initial reluctance of the French defense ministry to support the French commitment to lead the strengthened peacekeeping mission in Lebanon underscores the importance of ensuring military buy-in to peacekeeping.

Review the role of private contractors.

There are positive and negative aspects to private contractors that play a large role in a variety of areas, including development and policing. For instance, while the use of outside contractors avoids increased strain on U.S. personnel, retired personnel often lack access to DOD resources and are often less respected (often unfairly) than active duty military personnel. A USG-wide review of their performance and the development of standards and a code of ethics would be worthwhile. DOD has one such study underway regarding contractors on the battlefield.

UNITED NATIONS PEACEKEEPING OPERATIONS

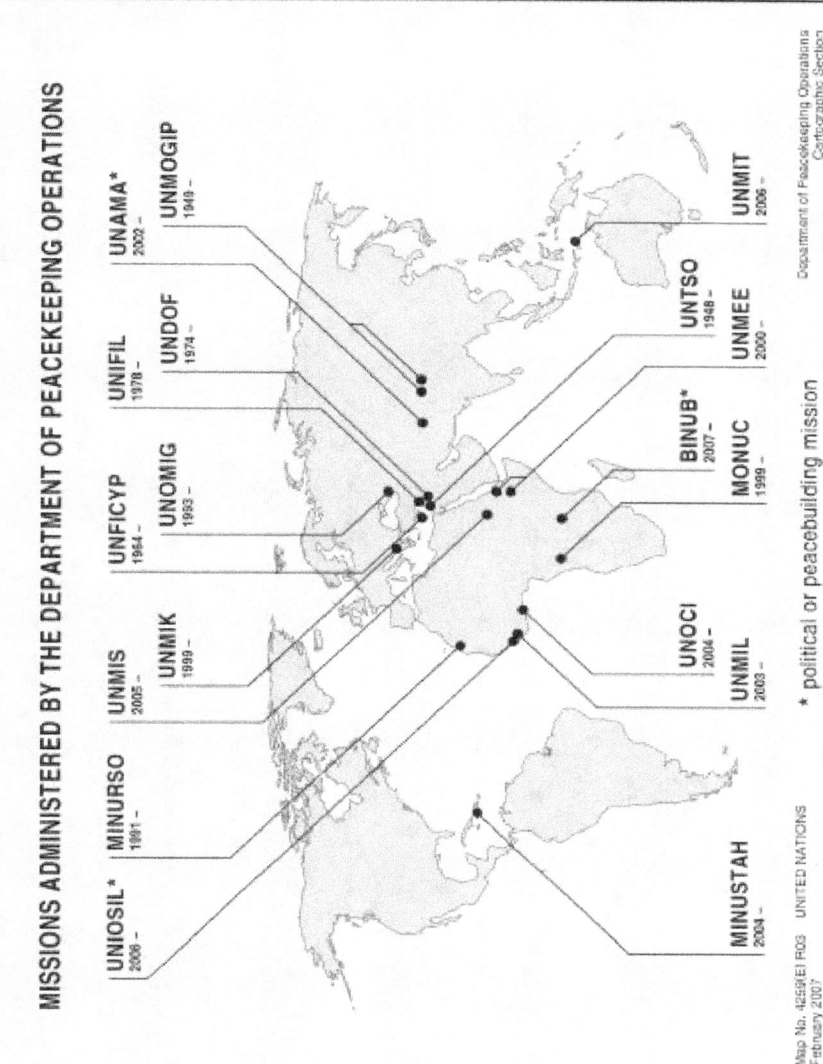

MISSIONS ADMINISTERED BY THE DEPARTMENT OF PEACEKEEPING OPERATIONS

UNIOSIL *
2006 –

MINURSO
1991 –

UNMIS
2005 –

UNMIK
1999 –

UNFICYP
1964 –

UNOMIG
1993 –

UNIFIL
1978 –

UNDOF
1974 –

UNAMA*
2002 –

UNMOGIP
1949 –

UNMIT
2006 –

UNTSO
1948 –

UNMEE
2000 –

BINUB*
2007 –

MONUC
1999 –

UNOCI
2004 –

UNMIL
2003 –

MINUSTAH
2004 –

* political or peacebuilding mission

Map No. 4259(E) R03   UNITED NATIONS
February 2007

Department of Peacekeeping Operations
Cartographic Section

Peacekeeping operations since 1948............61   61

Current peacekeeping operations..............16   15

Current peace operations directed and supported
by the Dept.of Peacekeeping Operations (DPKO)......18   18

PERSONNEL

Uniformed personnel............................82,685 *
(70,616 troops, 9,555 police and 2,514 military observers)

Countries contributing uniformed personnel......112115

International civilian personnel ....4,705 *

Total civilian personnel......................10,658 *

UN Volunteers...............................1,942 *

Total number of personnel serving in
15 peacekeeping operations......................99,990

Total number of personnel serving in
18 DPKO-led peace operations...................102,593 **

Total number of fatalities in
peace operations since 1948...................2,344 ***

FINANCIAL ASPECTS

Approved resources for the period
from 1 July 2006 to 30 June 2007.......   About 5.28 billion

Estimated total cost of operations
from 1948 to 30 June 2006.............   About $41.54 billion

Outstanding contributions to
peacekeeping (31 Jan. 2007) ....About $3.27.billion

---

* Numbers include 15 peacekeeping operations only. Statistics for three special political and/or peacebuilding missions—UNAMA, UNIOSIL and BINUB—directed and supported by DPKO can be found at http://www.un.org/Depts/dpko/dpko/ppmb.pdf

** This figure includes the total number of uniformed and civilian personnel serving in 15 peacekeeping operations and three DPKO-led special political and/or peacebuilding missions—UNAMA, UNIOSIL and BINUB.

*** Includes fatalities for all UN peace operations.

CURRENT PEACEKEEPING OPERATIONS

Mission	Established	Troops	Military Observers	Police	International Civilians	Local Civilians	UN Volunteers	Total Personnel	Fatalities	Budget (US$)
UNTSO	May 1948	0	152	0	111	117	0	380	48	29,961,200 (2006)
UNMOGIP	January 1949	0	44	0	19	46	0	109	11	7,919,100 (2006)
UNFICYP	March 1964	850	0	65	36	105	0	1,056	176	46,270,400
UNDOF	June 1974	1,042	0	0	41	95	0	1,178	42	39,865,200
UNIFIL	March 1978	13,024	0	0	202	308	0	13,534	260	350,866,600*
MINURSO	April 1991	28	195	6	100	137	24	490	14	45,935,000
UNOMIG	August 1993	0	126	12	100	184	1	423	11	33,377,900
UNMIK	June 1999	0	36	2,025	484	2,008	141	4,694	47	217,962,000
MONUC	November 1999	16,594	713	1,029	951	2,023	598	21,908	105	1,094,247,900
UNMEE	July 2000	1,594	202	0	144	197	62	2,199	17	137,385,100
UNMIL	September 2003	13,841	214	1,201	527	925	240	16,948	90	714,877,300
UNOCI	April 2004	7,854	200	1,187	382	535	232	10,390	31	472,889,300
MINUSTAH	June 2004	7,023	0	1,813	452	734	165	10,187	25	489,207,100
UNMIS	March 2005	8,766	599	662	922	2,398	186	13,533	18	1,079,534,400
UNMIT	August 2006	0	33	1,555	234	846	293	2,961	1	170,221,100**
Total:		70,616	2,514	9,555	4,705	10,658	1,942	99,990	896	About $5.28 billion***

UNTSO - UN Truce Supervision Organization
UNMOGIP - UN Military Observer Group in India and Pakistan
UNFICYP - UN Peacekeeping Force in Cyprus
UNDOF - UN Disengagement Observer Force
UNIFIL - UN Interim Force in Lebanon
MINURSO - UN Mission for the Referendum in Western Sahara
UNOMIG - UN Observer Mission in Georgia
UNMIK - UN Interim Administration Mission in Kosovo

MONUC - UN Organization Mission in the Dem. Rep. of the Congo
UNMEE - United Nations Mission in Ethiopia and Eritrea
UNMIL - United Nations Mission in Liberia
UNOCI - United Nations Operation in Côte d'Ivoire
MINUSTAH - United Nations Stabilization Mission in Haiti
UNMIS - United Nations Mission in the Sudan
UNMIT - United Nations Integrated Mission in Timor-Leste

*Commitment authority for 1 July 2006 to 31 March 2007.

**Commitment authority for 25 August to 31 March 2007.

***Includes requirements for the support account for peacekeeping operations and the UN Logistics Base in Brindisi (Italy). (See document A/C.5/61/18)

NOTE: UNTSO and UNMOGIP are funded from the United Nations regular biennial budget. Costs to the United Nations of the other current operations are financed from their own separate accounts on the basis of legally binding assessments on all Member States. For these missions, budget figures are for one year (07/06-06/07) unless otherwise specified. For information on United Nations political missions, see DPI/2166/Rev.45 also available on the web at http://www.un.org/Depts/dpko/dpko/ppbm.pdf.

Prepared by the Peace and Security Section of the United Nations Department of Public Information, in consultation with the Department of Peacekeeping Operations, Peacekeeping Financing Division of the Office of Programme Planning, Budget and Accounts, and the Department of Political Affairs — DPI/1634/Rev.70/Rev.1 — April 2007